Carving Caricature Pins & Bolos

By Gary Batte

Fox Chapel Publishing Co. Inc.

1970 Broad Street • East Petersburg, PA 17520 • www.foxchapelpublishing.com

Acknowledgments

◆

I would like to thank my wife, Sue, for her continued support in the preparation of this, my third carving book. I deeply appreciate her encouragement and advice on designs, color choices and finished projects. I also appreciate the assistance of my carver friend Dean Walden of Richardson, Texas, who consulted with me on bolo carving and furnished materials. I thank the number of book sellers who were consulted by the publisher regarding the potential of a book such as this: Wayne Edmonson of MDI Woodcarvers; Bernie Frigon of Valley Road Woodcarvers; Pam Johnston of Mountain Woodcarvers; Kathleen Schuck of Wood 'n Things; and Larry Yudis of The Woodcraft Shop. I appreciate their positive comments and encouragement.

◆

Copyright ©2001, Fox Chapel Publishing Company, Inc.

Carving Caricature Pins and Bolos is a brand new work, first published in 2001 by Fox Chapel Publishing Company, Inc. The patterns contained herein are copyrighted by the author. Readers may make three copies of these patterns for personal use and may make any number of projects based on these patterns. The patterns themselves, however, are not to be duplicated for resale or distribution under any circumstances. Any such copying is a violation of copyright laws.

Publisher:	Alan Giagnocavo
Editor:	Ayleen Stellhorn
Desktop Specialist:	Linda L. Eberly, Eberly Designs Inc.
Cover Photography:	Robert Polett
Interior Photography:	Robert Polett/Gary Batte
Cover Design:	Lori Schlossman

ISBN 1–56523–137–6
Library of Congress Card Number 2001088512
Manufactured in Korea
10 9 8 7 6 5 4 3 2 1

To order your copy of this book,
please send the cover price
plus $3.00 shipping to:
Fox Books
1970 Broad Street
East Petersburg, PA 17520

Or visit us on the web at
www.foxchapelpublishing.com

Table of Contents

About the Author iv

Introduction 1

Chapter One: Getting Started

Tools and Materials 2

Painting and Antiquing 3

Hardware 4

Chapter Two: Carving Pins

How-to Carving Demonstration: Uncle Sam 5

Patterns 8

Hot Lips	8	Witch-O'-Lantern	32
Hearts Abound	9	Witch-on-a-Stick	33
Luv Bug	10	Turkey Gobbler	34
Smiley Shamrock	11	Early American	35
Mr. Shamrock	12	Frosty	36
Lucky O'Casey	13	Silver Bells	37
Paddy O'Malley	14	Santa Mouse	38
Flop-Eared Bunny	15	Housetop Santa	39
Bucky Bunny	16	Jolly Santa	40
Easter Egg	17	Santa's Elf	41
Easter Chick	18	Rudolph	42
Ducky Rabbit	19	Sweet Treat	43
Zoomer	20	Merry Melon	44
Liberty Bell	21	Core-etta	45
Boomer	22	Hootie	46
Ozark Scarecrow	23	Busy Bee	47
Texas Scarecrow	24	Sunflower	48
Ghostie Goblin	25	Apple Samplers	49
Spook	26	Tommy Tomato	50
Dopey Ghost	27	Ribbit	51
Notta Bird	28	Man In the Moon	52
Goofy Jack	29	Speed-O	53
Scared Jack	30	Toadstool	54
Happy Jack	31	Fun Flower	55

Chapter Three: Carving Bolos

How-to Carving Demonstration: Cowpoke Bolo 56

Patterns 60

Cowboy Boot	60	Corky the Clown Bolo	64
Crazy Cow Bolo	61	Wild West Rabbit Bolo	66
Winking Santa Bolo	62	Home Sweet Home Bolo	67
Barfy Buzzard	63		

About the Author

Gary and his wife, Sue, reside in Stephenville, Texas. A carver since childhood, Gary is self-taught and likes to carve caricatures because they are fun and make people smile. His unique style incorporates humor and an understanding of caricature design.

Since retiring from the USDA Natural Resources Conservation Service in 1994, Gary spends more time carving, teaching, writing and exhibiting his works. He has won numerous awards, including first places at the International Woodcarvers Congress and Best of Show at the Texas Championship Woodcarving Show. His carvings have been exhibited at numerous galleries, museums and universities, including the George Bush Presidential Library and Museum and the National Woodcarving Museum. Gary's carvings have been featured in *Woodcarving Illustrated, Western Horseman, Wood, Art of the West* and *Chip Chats* magazines. His carvings can be found in many private collections throughout the United States.

Gary Batte

Gary has published two previous books: *Carving Crazy Critters* and *Carving Critters, Cowboys and Other Characters.* He also co-authored *The Full Moon Saloon* and *Carving the CCA Circus* with other members of the Caricature Carvers of America.

Gary is a founding member of the CCA, a group dedicated to promoting the art of caricature carving. He is also a member of the Texas Woodcarvers Guild, The National Woodcarvers Association, and the Affiliated Woodcarvers, Ltd.

Introduction

Welcome to *Carving Caricature Pins and Bolos.* Pins and bolos have many decorative uses, including the celebration of holidays, seasons and other events. Many carving club members like to wear hand-carved pins and bolos during club-sponsored activities such as carving shows and regular meetings.

The projects in this book can be carved quickly and require only small pieces of wood, a few tools and some paint. Pins and bolos can be of any style; however, most of these projects reflect my caricature background.

Because many of these projects require similar techniques, I did not include complete instructions for carving each pin or bolo. Instead, the carving and fin-ishing process for several examples are described in detail at the beginning of the pins and bolos chapters. The remainder of the projects include pertinent instructions for each.

All of the projects have a flat back, a few are carved "in-the-round" except for the flat side where the pin backing or bolo backing is attached, and others are flat relief variations. Some of the pin projects will also make good bolos, and some of the bolo projects will do well as pins. Nearly all will make good refrigerator magnets. They also make great gifts.

Have fun!
Gary Batte

Getting Started

Carving pins and bolos is fun and rewarding. These small projects are quickly made by carvers of all skill levels, making them ideal gifts for family and friends. They are also perfect items to sell at carving and craft shows. The whimsical caricature designs are sure to bring a smile to any recipient's face. Each pattern presented in this book can be carved "as is" or altered to reflect your own personality and style.

Before you begin, read through this basic information. The notes here will help to get you started and answer some basic questions on how to make caricature pins and bolos.

TOOLS AND MATERIALS

Wood Choice

Although any type of wood can be used to carve pins and

Knives and gouges are used to carve the pieces in this book.

bolos, I recommend basswood for the projects in this book. Good quality wood is always a sound investment. I prefer northern basswood because it is easy to carve and takes detail well.

Basswood can be purchased in thin stock, such as ½–¾ in., which is ideal for pins and bolos. Basswood, as well as other carving woods, can be found at craft shops, stores specializing in woodcraft supplies, carving shows and mail order suppliers. When purchasing basswood, look for white wood with few imperfections. Avoid wood from the center of the tree (identified by small annual growth rings) because it is harder and more difficult to carve. Jelutong is a good second choice of wood for this type of carving.

Carving Tools

Five-inch palm tools and a 1¼ in. to 1¾ in. straight-edge blade carving knife are ideal for carving pins and bolos. About one-fourth of these pins and bolos can be carved with just a knife. Look for the "knife only" logo that marks these projects.

The use of other tools in addition to a knife will make the job of carving easier. Choose a tool that will make the cut you desire. For example, if a U-shaped cut is needed, select a gouge with the proper blade shape (sweep) and width. The sweep number is usually embossed on the shaft. The larger the number, the flatter the sweep. Tool catalogs usually specify the width of the cutting edge in millimeters.

A veiner is U-shaped and is sometimes called a "deep U-gouge." Veiners are useful in areas such as eye sockets and other areas where gouges and knives aren't as efficient or can't reach.

V-tools, also called parting tools, are good for creating hair texture and separations such as those between the arm and the body.

A skew chisel has a flat, angular blade and is useful for removing thin slices of wood in areas that are difficult to reach with a knife.

Tools List

1-½ in. or 1-¾ in. carving knife with a straight-edged blade	3 mm v-tool
	4 mm skew chisel
	10 mm skew chisel
2 mm veiner	#9, 6 mm straight gouge
3 mm veiner	#7, 8 mm straight gouge
4 mm veiner	#5, 10 mm straight gouge
5 mm veiner	#9, 3 mm straight gouge
2 mm v-tool	

Additional Materials

The following materials are part of any well-stocked carving studio.

- Ruler: A flexible, transparent plastic ruler is ideal.
- Pencil and eraser: I recommend a no. 2 pencil with an eraser, although sometimes an art gum eraser does a better job of cleaning up leftover or unwanted marks.
- Plain white paper: Typing or computer paper will do for tracing patterns.
- Light box (optional): A light box—commercial or homemade—is useful in transferring patterns from the pages of this book to a sheet of paper.
- Band saw or scroll saw: Either machine will cut the curves involved in these projects. Because most of the projects are small, a ⅛ in. wide, 16-teeth-per-inch blade works nicely. A hand-held coping saw can also be used.
- Carving glove: Try a cut-resistant mesh-type glove.
- Thumb guard: Leather thumb guards are available. Wrapping the thumb with tape works also well.

Safety

Safety is always important, regardless of the type of carving you are doing. Because most of the projects in this book are small, the chances of injury are increased.

Normally, the pieces are held in one hand while being carved with the other. I recommend wearing a cut-resistant mesh-type carving glove on the hand holding the piece and a thumb guard on the thumb of the opposite hand. A leather apron provides added protection. Safety gear such as this can be purchased at any carving supply store.

As always, use good lighting and take breaks often. Don't carve if you are tired or distracted.

Sharpening

Although this book does not cover sharpening techniques, I urge you to become proficient in sharpening your tools before attempting any of the projects in this book. This is especially important because of the many small and detailed cuts required with smaller tools.

Various types of power sharpeners will speed up the sharpening process. I use a power sharpener that has a grinding wheel, two leather-covered wheels and a buffing wheel for most of my sharpening. I have moved to using power sharpeners because of their speed; however, I still rely on hand sharpening for some of my tools—especially the smaller ones that are more difficult to sharpen. I use diamond hand sharpeners and leather strops for some of my very smallest tools. Try a sharpening compound such as Zam™ or Yellowstone™ to charge leather strops and buffing wheels.

PAINTING AND ANTIQUING

Carving is just the first step in completing the projects in this book. Painting puts the finishing touches on an attractive and humorous carving. Take some time to learn painting techniques from an experienced carver and practice them diligently on a piece of scrap wood before painting your carving.

Using Acrylic Paints

To prepare your carving for paint, lightly sand the back (flat) side. Brush the carving with a brush, such as a toothbrush, to remove loose wood particles. If it is especially dirty, use an art gum eraser to remove smudges and pencil marks. Brushing with water and dishwashing detergent can also be done if necessary. This will also help to remove "fuzzies" and small wood particles. Be sure to let the carving dry thoroughly before painting. With acrylic paints, there is no need to seal the wood before painting.

I used both tube and liquid acrylic paints—depending on

the colors desired—for the projects in this book. Acrylics are easy to use, fast drying and clean up easily with water and dish-washing detergent or a mild abrasive soap.

Using a brush, mix the paint and the water to achieve a watery stain. I usually apply one coat; then, if the paint looks too thin, I apply another coat. I like my carvings to have a stained look with the wood grain showing through the paint. I generally use less water with metallic and white. These colors need a fuller strength to cover the wood adequately.

For flesh colors, I used Vermilion red watercolor paint blended with the flesh paint.

A disadvantage to using acrylics is that they have the tendency to run and bleed into unwanted areas. To minimize this, allow one area to dry before painting the area next to it. Also, use a small brush when painting near areas where the danger of running or bleeding exists. Make use of gravity to keep paint from running into unwanted areas by tilting the carving toward you or away from you as you paint.

Choosing Paint Brushes

I recommend that you buy the best quality brushes you can afford. The more expensive brushes do a better job and last longer. I like sable brushes the best, though there are also some good quality synthetic brushes available.

For the projects in this book, I used ¼ in. and ³⁄₁₆ in. flat square-end brushes and 2/0 and 3/0 round brushes.

Adding Details

I often use round or sharpened toothpicks to paint hard-to-reach areas, such as the corner of an eye. Painted dots can be

Acrylic paints and an antiquing mixture are used to finish the carvings.

added quickly and neatly by applying paint straight from the bottle with a round toothpick.

Fine-tipped pens are useful for adding final finishing details. Use them to outline the iris of an eye, color pupils and create lettering. I use a Pigma Micron, no. 005 pen, which is very fine, and heavier-lined nos. 03 and 05. These have quick-drying black waterproof ink.

Details can often be penciled in before painting begins and traced over with the black ink later. For example, on the Witch-o'-Lantern (page 32), I used a pencil to mark the eyes, nose, mouth and tooth before I began painting. The marks showed through the thin green paint. When the paint was dry, I traced over the lines with a black pen.

I also use a woodburner to add some details after the pieces are painted. Woodburners are ideal for lettering, stitches and button holes.

Antiquing

After the paint has dried, I seal the finished carvings with an antiquing mixture. This mixture protects the carvings and gives the paint a uniform tone.

Antiquing mixtures can be bought from carving supply stores, or you can make your own. Simply mix a ¼ in. by ½ in. ribbon of raw umber or burnt umber oil paint with 13 oz. of boiled linseed oil in a coffee can or similar container. Test the solution on a scrap piece of painted basswood (or whatever wood you used for your carving). Too much raw umber or burnt umber color in the mix will darken the acrylic paints excessively or bleed through them. Just enough will enhance the paints' finish and help to bring out details.

Apply the mixture to your carving with a brush and wipe off the excess with a soft cotton cloth. Let the carving dry for several days. Warning: Linseed oil is highly flammable. Properly dispose of oily rags to avoid spontaneous combustion. Store in a closed metal container until delivered to a hazardous materials collection center.

HARDWARE

Allow the carving to dry for about two days. Then attach a pin, magnet or bolo hardware to the back side. Use glue that is suitable for metal and wood, such as two-part epoxy. Hardware attachments can be found at local craft stores or stores that sell rock cutting and polishing (lapidary) supplies.

Carving Pins

Several carving styles were used for the pin projects in this book. Some were carved using variations of the "flat-plane" style, while others were carved "in-the-round," except for the back, which was left flat.

Pin backings are available in several sizes. For the projects in this book, 1 inch and 1¼ inch pins were used. You can easily turn any of the pins in this chapter into refrigerator magnets by substituting a magnet in place of the pin. Secure the pin or magnet to the back of the carving with epoxy glue. Some of the pin projects are also suitable for bolos.

When designing your own pin carving or altering the patterns included in this chapter, be sure to make the carving large enough to accommodate the size of the pin backing that you plan to attach. Also make sure that the piece of wood you select is at least as thick as the thickest part of the carving. Use carbon paper to trace the outline and details onto the piece of wood before you saw the rough blank.

The pin project that follows provides detailed carving instructions and photos, which will be helpful in carving many of the other pins in this chapter.

Uncle Sam

Finished Size
¼ in. thick by 2 in. wide by 3⅜ in. tall

Carving Notes
As with several other projects in this book, *Uncle Sam* is carved in the three-dimensional relief style made famous by my

Uncle Sam pin

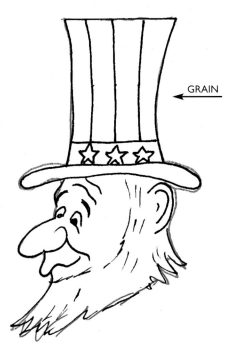

GRAIN

Pattern
(100%)
© 2001 Gary Batte

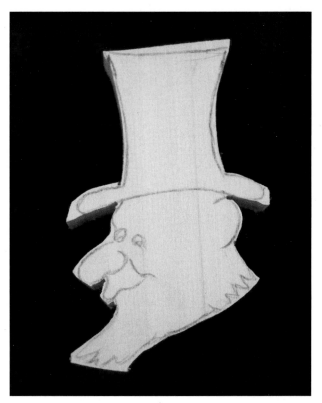

Photo 1 – Bandsaw the blank.

friend Harley Schmitgen of Blue Earth, Minnesota. When completed, the head is turned at a slight angle—about 20 degrees to the left—while the back remains flat.

This style of relief carving is different from flat relief in that it allows more details to be included. It offers an alternative method of carving and will require new skills. The carver must see the carving in a different perspective than that used in flat relief. Uncle Sam's face is slightly turned and only portions of the right eye, nostril and mouth are showing. The left eye is carved so that it appears to follow the viewer. Because this is a caricature, several features are also exaggerated: The sizes of the nose, ear and lip are larger than normal; the right eye is slightly smaller than the left.

First, use carbon paper to transfer the features to the surface of the wood before band sawing the side view. (See Photo 1.) Next, reduce the thickness of the hat crown. Now round the back portion of the crown and brim. Round the front portion of the hat at a wider angle (about 35 degrees) than the back (about 20 degrees).

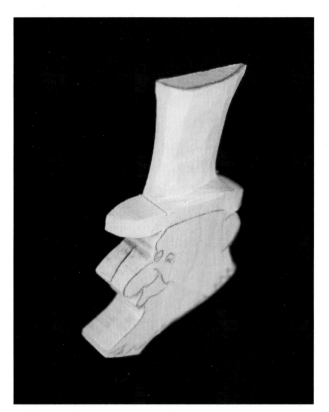

Chapter One

Photo 2 – Pencil in the center line.

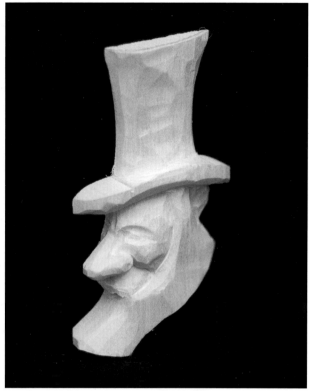

Photo 3 – Begin carving the basic shape.

Mark a center line along the top of the nose. Carve the nose so that it angles outward at about 20 degrees. (See Photo 2.)

Carve the nose and shape the cheek. Be sure to leave enough wood for the beard.

Round the beard, mouth and forehead. Round the hair at the back half of the carving, remembering to leave wood for the ear. Round these features at approximately the same angles as the hat so the perspective remains true.

Carve the left eye socket and the eye. Then carve only about one quarter of the right eye and the socket next to the nose. (See Photo 3.)

Carve the stars on the hat in relief. Using a small v-tool, carve shallow separations between the stripes on the hat. This will show separation between the colors and help to prevent the paint from running together.

Sand the back of your finished carving and paint it with the suggested colors.

Suggested Colors

Face: Flesh tone with vermilion watercolor blended on the nose, cheek, lips and tip of the ear

Hair: White

Eye: White with cobalt blue/raw umber mix for the iris; pupil is a black with a white dot

Hat: Napthol red light/raw umber mix, white and navy blue

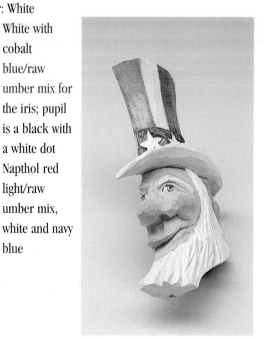

Hot Lips

Shown larger than actual size

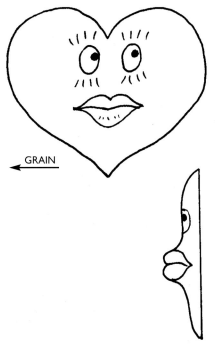

← GRAIN

Pattern
(100%)
© 2001 Gary Batte

Finished Size
⅜ in. thick by 2³⁄₂₆ in. wide by 1¾ in. tall

Carving Notes
Remove wood from all sides of the lips with a 5 mm veiner and a knife. Round the edges of the lips and the heart. Separate the lips with the knife and shape the lips. Make a stop cut around the eyes with the tip of the knife. Round the eyeballs with the knife and the skew chisel.

Suggested Colors
Heart: Napthol red light/white mix
Eyes: white and black with white highlights
Lashes: black ink
Lips: Napthol red light/raw umber mix

Hearts Abound

Shown larger than actual size

Shown larger than actual size

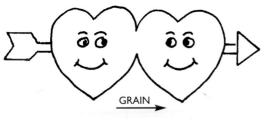

Pattern
(100%)
© 2001 Gary Batte

Finished Size

⅜ in. thick by 2⅞ in. wide by 1 in. tall

Carving Notes

Carve wood from each side of the arrow to reduce it to ⅛ in. thickness. Slightly bevel the edges of the arrow. Round the edges of the hearts.

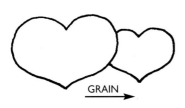

Pattern
(100%)
© 2001 Gary Batte

Finished Size

³⁄₁₆ in. thick by 1¾ in. wide by 1 in. tall

Carving Notes

Use a knife to remove any saw marks from the edges of the blank. Then make a stop cut along the side of the large heart where it is attached to the small heart. Carve the small heart until it is about one half of the thickness of the large heart. Round the edges of both hearts and smooth the surfaces.

Suggested Colors for both projects

Hearts: Napthol red light/raw umber mix

Luv Bug

Shown larger than actual size

Pattern
(100%)
© 2001 Gary Batte

Finished Size
¼ in. thick by 1¾ in. wide by 1¼ in. tall

Carving Notes

The grain must run in the same direction as the bug's antenna. Carve the antenna down to ⅛ in. thickness. Carve a separation between the head and the body; then round the head and the body separately. Round the legs. Carve the stem of the antenna; then round the end.

Suggested Colors

Body: jubilee green/raw umber mix
Hearts: Napthol red light/raw umber mix outlined with black ink
Feet and antenna: black
Head: burnt umber with black ink for the eye and the mouth

Smiley Shamrock

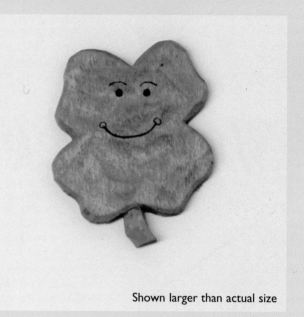

Shown larger than actual size

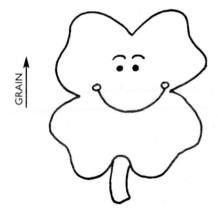

Pattern
(100%)
© 2001 Gary Batte

Finished Size

⅛ in. thick by 1¾ in. wide by 2 in. tall

Carving Notes

Smooth the surface with a knife or a 10 mm skew chisel. Round the edges and stem with a knife.

Suggested Colors

Shamrock: jubilee green/raw umber mix

Face: black ink

Mr. Shamrock

Knife Only

Shown larger than actual size

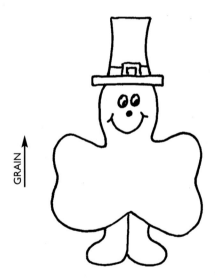

GRAIN

Pattern
(100%)

© 2001 Gary Batte

Finished Size
½ in. thick by 1¾ in. wide by 2⅝ in. tall

Carving Notes
Round the hat brim and crown, leaving enough thickness for the band and the buckle. Carve the buckle and the band by first making a knife stop cut along the edge, then removing wood adjacent to the cut. Round the edges of the body and feet.

Suggested Colors
Shamrock: jubilee green/raw umber mix
Eyes: black and white
Nose and mouth: black ink
Hat: Christmas green with jubilee green band and solid gold buckle
Feet: burnt umber

"Lucky" O'Casey

Shown larger than actual size

Pattern
(100%)
© 2001 Gary Batte

GRAIN

Finished Size

⅜ in. thick by 2 in. wide by 2¾ in. tall

Carving Notes

Carve this project in relief. (See *Uncle Sam* on page 5 for a description of 3-D relief carving.)

Suggested Colors

Face: flesh tone with Vermilion red watercolor blended on the cheeks, the end of the nose, the tip of the ear and the lips

Teeth: white

Eyes: white with cobalt blue/raw umber irises and black ink pupils

Beard and eye brows: burnt sienna

Hat: Christmas green with Jubilee green band and shamrock

Paddy O'Malley

Shown larger than actual size

Pattern
(100%)
© 2001 Gary Batte

Finished Size

⅝ in. thick by 1⅜ in. wide by 3¼ in. tall

Carving Notes

Band saw the basic shape then rough out the side view. Round the hat crown and the brim. Make a stop cut on each pocket line. Carve the surplus from the front and lower half of each arm down to the pocket lines.

Round the arms, legs, body and shoes. Carve separations between the legs and the feet and between the arms and the body..

Carve a nose with a gouge or veiner. Use a 3 mm veiner to define the beard. Round the mouth, the cheeks and the forehead. Carve small eye sockets and define the eyes with a pencil. Round the beard and carve the mouth.

Carve the details on the clothing. Carve the buttons before carving the straps on the trousers. Finish carving the hat details, including the shamrock and the hat band. Carve the beard with a v-tool.

Suggested Colors

Hat and trousers: Christmas green
Shirt and shamrock on hat: jubilee green/raw umber mix
Buttons and shoes: burnt umber
Beard and eye brows: burnt sienna
Face: flesh with vermilion watercolor blended on the lips, nose and cheeks

Flop-Eared Bunny

Shown larger than actual size

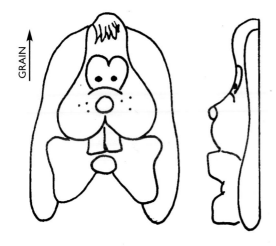

Pattern
(100%)
© 2001 Gary Batte

GRAIN

Finished Size

½ in. thick by 1⅝ in. wide by 2¼ in. tall

Carving Notes

Remove wood around the head and the bow tie; leave the ears ¹⁄₁₆ in. thick. Carve the teeth and the bow tie, in that order. Remove wood from the upper part of the head (above the nose) and round the head. Carve the separations between the teeth and the wrinkles in the bow tie with a v-tool. Make a stop cut around the perimeter of the eyes. Round the eyeballs slightly, giving each a convex shape.

Suggested Colors

Head: burnt umber
Nose: pink (white/Napthol red light mix)
Eyes: white, black
Teeth: white
Bow tie: pink with denim dots applied with a cut-off round toothpick

Bucky Bunny

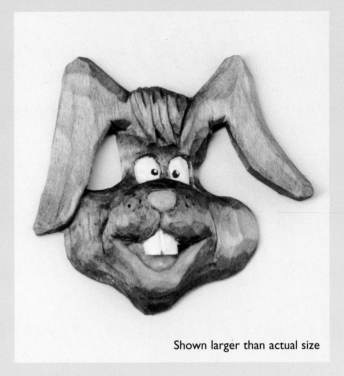

Shown larger than actual size

GRAIN

Pattern
(100%)
© 2001 Gary Batte

Finished Size
⅜ in. thick by 2⅜ in. wide by 2⅛ in. tall

Carving Notes

Carve everything above the nose down to ⁵⁄₃₂ in. thick. Further reduce the thickness by carving around the hair and between the hair and the snout. Thin the ears to about ³⁄₁₆ in.

Round the snout, leaving wood for the teeth, chin and mouth. Carve wood from around the teeth. Carve the separation between the right ear and the face. Shape the ears and round the head. Shape the chin with a gouge and round the mouth area.

Carve the mouth by first making a stop cut around the edge; then hollow out the opening, leaving wood for the tongue. Round the tongue with a knife tip or a 3 mm skew chisel. Shape the bottom lip.

Carve a stop cut around the eyes with a knife; then round the eyeballs. Carve the separations in the hair and between the teeth with a v-tool. Slightly round the edges of the teeth.

Suggested Colors
Head: very thin black
Tongue: Napthol red light
Nose and lips: medium flesh

Easter Egg

Knife
Only

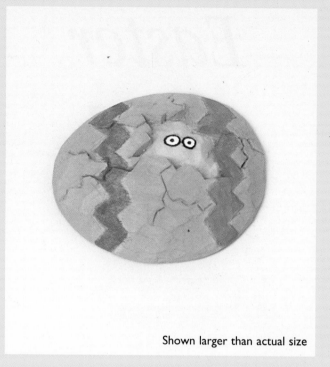

Shown larger than actual size

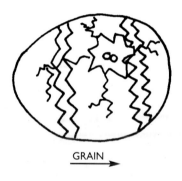

Pattern
(100%)
© 2001 Gary Batte

GRAIN →

Finished Size

¼ in. thick by 1⅝ in. wide by 1⁵⁄₁₆ in. high

Carving Notes

Round the egg. With a sharp knife tip, make a stop cut ¹⁄₁₆ in. deep along the edges of the hole in the egg. Hollow the egg out to the depth of the cut. Carve the cracks.

Suggested Colors

Egg: denim blue, orange, bright red
Chick: yellow
Eyes: white and black

Boomer

Shown larger than actual size

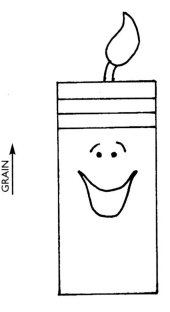

Pattern
(100%)
© 2001 Gary Batte

GRAIN

Finished Size

1 in. wide by ¼ in. thick by 3 in. tall

Carving Notes

Round the firecracker, leaving the fuse ⅛ thick and the flame ³⁄₁₆ in. thick. Taper the flame to the top. Make separation cuts on each side of the bands.

Suggested Colors

Firecracker: Napthol red/raw umber mix, white, navy

Fuse: black

Flame: yellow with an orange tip

Facial design: black ink

Ozark Scarecrow

Shown larger than actual size

GRAIN

Pattern
(100%)

© 2001 Gary Batte

Finished Size

⅜ thick by 1⅜ in. wide by 3 in. tall

Carving Notes

Round the hat and the brim. Shape the arms, the legs, the straw hands and the feet. Carve the arm separations with a knife and a v-tool. Use the v-tool to detail the straw arms and feet.

Suggested Colors

Head: antique white

Eyes and mouth: black ink

Overalls: cobalt blue/raw umber mix

Buckles: iridescent silver

Shirt: Napthol red light/raw umber mix

Straw hands and feet: yellow oxide/white mix

Stitches: woodburner

Texas Scarecrow

Shown larger than actual size

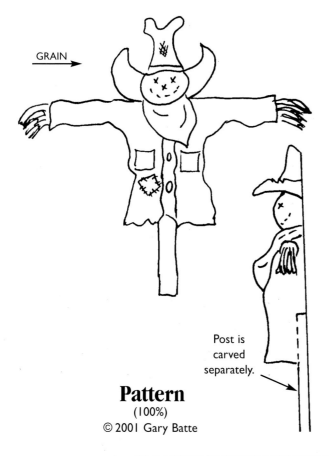

GRAIN →

Post is carved separately.

Pattern
(100%)
© 2001 Gary Batte

Finished Size

½ in. thick by 3¼ in. wide by 3 in. tall

Carving Notes

Carve the excess wood from the front of the shirt, leaving wood for the bandanna. Carve excess wood from the front of the hat crown; round the brim and the crown. Round the arms and the body of the shirt, leaving wood for the straw hands. Round the head and shape the bandanna. Carve the straw hands with a v-tool. Carve a flat, vertical groove ⅛ in. deep by ³⁄₁₆ in. wide by ½ in. long in the lower center of the back. Glue a 1¼-in.-long stick to fit the groove. It will extend ¾ of an inch below the shirt.

Suggested Colors

Head: antique white

Eyes and mouth: black ink

Shirt: cobalt blue/raw umber mix

Bandanna: Napthol red light/raw umber mix with white dots

Hat: black

Support stick: burnt umber

Ghostie Goblin

Shown larger than actual size

Pattern
(100%)
© 2001 Gary Batte

GRAIN

Finished Size

¼ in. thick by 2⅜ in. wide by 3¼ in. tall

Carving Notes

Round the ghost to achieve a convex shape. Mark the jack-o'-lantern. Carve the separation between the head and the body. Define the arms with a 3 mm veiner. Remove wood from around the jack-o'-lantern; then round it. Carve several grooves on the surface and at the base of the stem.

Suggested Colors

Ghost: white

Facial features of ghost and jack-o'-lantern: black ink

Jack-o'-lantern: pumpkin and hunter green/raw umber mix

Notta Bird

Shown larger than actual size

Pattern
(100%)
© 2001 Gary Batte

GRAIN →

Finished Size
¼ in. thick by 3½ in. wide by 1⅝ in. tall

Carving Notes
Thin the wings to a ⅛ in. thickness. Carve the body down to ³⁄₁₆ in. thick; leave the head the maximum thickness of the wood. Round the body and the ears. Shape the feet. Remove a small amount of wood from the inside of each ear with a veiner.

Suggested Colors
Eyes: white and black
Body: black
Mouth line and tooth: white

Goofy Jack

Shown larger than actual size

Pattern
(100%)
© 2001 Gary Batte

GRAIN

Finished Size

⅜ in. thick. by 2⅛ in. wide by 2⅛ in. tall

Carving Notes

Begin carving the jack-o'-lantern by first reducing the stem—except for the flared area at the point of attachment—to ⅛ in. thick. Round the piece to a convex shape. Round the stem and carve separations at the point of attachment.

Carve the eyes and nose by first making a stop cut with a knife about $\frac{1}{32}$ in. to $\frac{1}{16}$ in. deep around the perimeter of each. Make a second cut inside the first; angle this second cut toward the first cut and remove the wedge of wood created by the two cuts. Round the inside with a knife or skew chisel.

Carve the mouth in a similar fashion, leaving wood for the tooth. Carve smile lines at each corner of the mouth with the knife point. Carve the curved grooves of the pumpkin with a 3 mm v-tool; then smooth and round the grooves with a knife or skew chisel.

Suggested Colors

Jack-o'-lantern: pumpkin with black and white eyes
Stem: hunter green/raw umber mix

Scared Jack

Shown larger than actual size

Pattern
(100%)
© 2001 Gary Batte

GRAIN

Finished Size

⅜ in. thick by 2 in. wide by 2⅝ in. tall

Carving Notes

Follow the instructions for Goofy Jack on page 29, except hollow out an open mouth with a 5 mm veiner.

Suggested Colors

Jack-o'-lantern: pumpkin with black and white eyes
Stem: hunter green/raw umber

Happy Jack

Shown larger than actual size

Finished Size

⅜ in. thick by 2⅛ in. wide by 2½ in. tall

Carving Notes

Refer to *Goofy Jack* on page 29. The carving procedure is the same with the following exceptions: Make stop cuts around each side of the tongue and thin the rest of the tongue down to ³⁄₁₆ in. Round the pumpkin and the tongue. Remove some wood from behind the tongue. Carve the mouth and the teeth. Remove wood to about a ¹⁄₁₆ in. depth inside the mouth. Carve a groove in the center of the tongue and round the edges of the groove with a knife.

Suggested Colors

Jack-o'-lantern: pumpkin with black and white eyes
Stem: hunter green/raw umber mix
Tongue: Napthol red light/raw umber mix

GRAIN

Pattern
(100%)
© 2001 Gary Batte

Witch-o'-Lantern

Shown larger than actual size

GRAIN →

Pattern
(100%)
© 2001 Gary Batte

Finished Size

¼ in. thick by 2¼ in. wide by 3⅛ in. tall

Carving Notes

First make a stop cut about ¹⁄₁₆ in. deep along the bottom of the hat brim. Remove the wood beneath this cut and carve the pumpkin as in *Goofy Jack* on page 29. Shape the hat crown and brim. Carve the hatband, buckle and other hat details.

Suggested Colors

Pumpkin: jubilee green/raw umber mix

Facial details: black ink

Hat: black with violet band and metallic gold buckle

Eyes and tooth: white with black dots

Witch-on-a-Stick

Shown larger than actual size

Finished Size

½ in. thick by 4¼ in. wide by 3⅜ in. tall

Carving Notes

Make sure that the grain runs in the same direction as the broom handle. Carve the broom first. Then carve the hand and the arm, leaving the knee and the leg angling slightly outward. Round the rest of the body. Carve the face angling toward the end of the nose. Round the facial features. Carve the hair at an angle toward the side of the head. Round the hat brim and the crown. Detail the hand, foot, face and hair.

Suggested Colors

Cloak and hat: Dioxazine purple
Skin: Jubilee green/raw umber mix
Hair: white streaked with black
Broom straw: yellow oxide
Broom handle: burnt umber

GRAIN →

Pattern
(100%)
© 2001 Gary Batte

Frosty

Shown larger than actual size

Pattern
(100%)
© 2001 Gary Batte

GRAIN

Finished Size

½ in. thick by 1¹³⁄₁₆ in. wide by 2⅞ in. tall

Carving Notes

Bandsaw the front view. Carve the body down to a ¼ in. thickness, except for the left arm and the package. Further carve the right arm and head down to ⅛ in. thick. Reduce the package down to ⅛ in. thick, leaving ¹⁄₁₆ in. thickness on top for the bow. Shape and round the left arm to curve around the package. Use a 3 mm veiner, a knife and a small v-tool to carve the ribbon details.

Suggested Colors

Body: white

Belt, buttons, eyes, nose, mouth, gloves: black

Cap: Napthol red light/raw umber mix with white trim

Buckle: iridescent silver

Scarf: sweetheart blush and hunter green

Package: Christmas green and Napthol red light/raw umber mix

Silver Bells

Shown larger than actual size

GRAIN →

Pattern
(100%)
© 2001 Gary Batte

Finished Size
¼ in. thick by 2¼ wide by 1¼ in. tall

Carving Notes
Remove the surplus wood from the front of the clappers, leaving them ⅛ in. thick. Round the clappers and the bells, leaving wood for the holly and the berries. Carve around the holly and the berries. Using a gouge, carve a flare on the lower part of each bell.

Suggested Colors
Bells: iridescent silver
Holly: Christmas green
Berries: Napthol red light

Santa Mouse

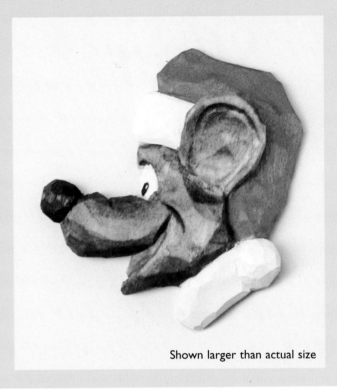

Shown larger than actual size

GRAIN →

Pattern
(100%)
© 2001 Gary Batte

Finished Size

½ in. thick by 2⅛ in. wide by 2¼ in. tall

Carving Notes

Carve surplus wood from the side of the cap, leaving the ear ¼ in. thick at the top. Carve the ball on the end of the cap. Reduce the nose to ¼ in. thick. Round the nose, the snout and the facial area.

Starting at the top of the ear, use a gouge to carve downward at an angle to the point of attachment. Hollow out the inside.

Carve the trim around the neck and on the cap. Carve the mouth, leaving wood for the tongue. Separate the tongue and the lower lip with a v-tool.

With a no. 9, 6 mm gouge, carve a shallow eye socket. Make a stop cut with the tip of a knife around the perimeter of the eye; then make another knife cut inside and adjacent to the first cut, removing a wedge of wood around inside edge of the eye. Round the eyeball.

Suggested Colors

Head: very thin black
Tongue: Napthol red light
Cap: sweetheart blush and white
Collar: white

Housetop Santa

Shown larger than actual size

GRAIN →

Pattern
(100%)
© 2001 Gary Batte

Finished Size
⁷⁄₁₆ in. thick by 2¼ in. wide by 2¼ in. tall

Carving Notes
Refer to *Uncle Sam* on page 5 and *Home Sweet Home* on page 67. Using the 3-D relief style, carve the Santa with his nose, mustache, hair and tassel protruding over the chimney. Carve the separations between the bricks with a v-tool.

Suggested Colors
Cap: Napthol red light/raw umber
    mix with white trim
Face: flesh tone with Vermilion
    red watercolor blended on
    nose
Chimney: orange bricks with very
    thin black trim around the
    top

Jolly Santa

Shown larger than actual size

Pattern
(100%)
© 2001 Gary Batte

GRAIN →

Finished Size

¼ in. thick by 1½ in. wide by 2¾ in. tall

Carving Notes

All of the carving on this pin is done entirely with a knife, except for the hair, which was carved with a small v-tool.

Trace the pattern, including details, onto the wood. Make a stop cut with a knife along the edges of details such as the coat trim, belt and buckle, gloves, cap and beard. Then remove wood from adjacent to these cuts to provide relief. Round the clothing details and nose; shape the cheek and forehead. Carve a slit for the closed eye. Shape the outside edges of the body, suit, gloves, boots and head.

Suggested Colors

Cap and suit: Napthol red light/raw umber mix with white trim

Belt and boot: black

Buckle: iridescent silver

Face: flesh tone with Vermilion red watercolor blended on the nose and cheeks

Hair: white

Santa's Elf

Shown larger than actual size

GRAIN →

Pattern
(100%)

© 2001 Gary Batte

Finished Size

¼ in. thick by 2¼ in. wide by 3⅜ in. tall

Carving Notes

Carve this pin in the same manner as the *Jolly Santa* project on page 40. Use a knife, small gouge and skew chisel to carve around the hammer.

Suggested Colors

Cap and shoe: Christmas green and white

Shirt: sweetheart blush

Beard: white

Face, arm, hand, leg: flesh with Vermilion red watercolor blended on the nose, cheeks, lips, eyelid, knuckles and elbow

Eye: white outlined with black ink

Iris: cobalt blue/raw umber iris with a black pupil

Hammer: burnt umber with iridescent silver

Rudolph

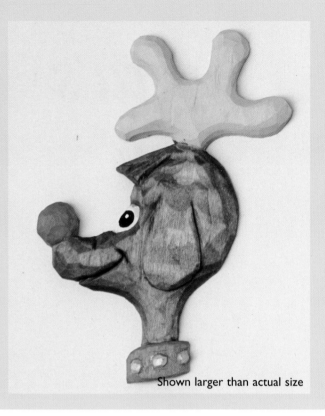

Shown larger than actual size

Pattern
(100%)
© 2001 Gary Batte

GRAIN →

Finished Size

¼ in. thick by 2½ in. wide by 3½ in. tall

Carving Notes

Carve the antlers to a ³⁄₁₆ in. thickness. Carve the head and the neck to a ⅛ in. thickness, leaving the nose, ear and collar ¼ in. thick. Round the edges of the antlers.

Round the nose and the collar, leaving enough wood for the ornaments. Define the ears with a knife and round the edges.

Carve the collar ornaments. Round the head and carve the mouth. Carve the eye socket with a no. 7,8 mm gouge; then carve the eye as explained in the *Santa Mouse* project on page 38. Carve the hair with a v-tool.

Suggested Colors

Head: burnt umber
Eye: white and black
Nose and collar: Napthol red light/raw umber mix
Collar decorations: iridescent silver
Antlers: antique white/raw umber mix

Sweet Treat

Shown larger than actual size

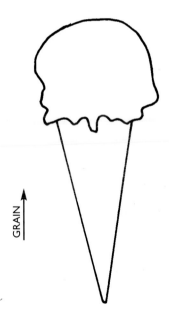

GRAIN

Pattern
(100%)
© 2001 Gary Batte

Finished Size

⅜ in. thick by 1⅜ in. wide by 3 in. tall

Carving Notes

Round the cone and the ice cream. Use a 3 mm veiner and the tip of a knife to carve the drippy edges. Make the waffle design on the cone with a woodburner after painting.

Suggested Colors

Ice cream: bright red/white mix
Cone: burnt umber with woodburned design

Merry Melon

Shown larger than actual size

GRAIN →

Pattern
(100%)
© 2001 Gary Batte

Finished Size
¼ in. thick by 2¾ in. wide by 1⅝ in. tall

Carving Notes
Starting at the bottom, remove the surplus wood toward the top, thinning the slice as you go. Carve teeth marks with 3 mm veiner.

Suggested Colors
Melon: hunter green, white, Napthol red light
Eyes, seeds and other features: black

Core-etta

Shown larger than actual size

GRAIN

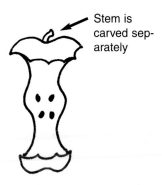

Stem is carved sep- arately

Pattern
(100%)
© 2001 Gary Batte

Finished Size
⅜ in. thick by ¾ in. wide by 1½ in. tall

Carving Notes
Round the ends with a knife. Use a 5 mm veiner to round the center part by removing small "bites." Make cuts along the edges of the ends with the same tool. Drill a ³⁄₃₂ in. hole in the large end and insert a stem carved from a ⅛ in. dowel.

Suggested Colors
Apple skin: Napthol red light/raw umber mix
Stem and seeds: burnt umber
Inside: natural wood

Hootie

Knife Only

Shown larger than actual size

GRAIN →

Pattern
(100%)
© 2001 Gary Batte

Finished Size

½ in. thick by 1¾ in. wide by 2⅜ in. tall

Carving Notes

After sawing out the front view, carve wood away from the front of the wings and on both sides of the belly and the head. Carve the beak. Next, round the head and the belly. Shape the feather tufts to resemble ears. Carve the eyes. Then, round the perch to the outside of each foot. Carve the feet and finish rounding the perch.

Suggested Colors

Body: raw umber with antique white belly

Eyes: black and white

Beak and feet: yellow oxide

Toe nails: black

Perch: very thin black

Busy Bee

Knife Only

Shown larger than actual size

GRAIN

Pattern
(100%)
© 2001 Gary Batte

Suggested Colors
⅜ in. thick by 1½ in. long by 1½ in. tall

Suggested Colors

Carve the wings down to ¹⁄₁₆ in. thick, except for the area of the legs, which will need to be about ⅛ in. thick. Carve the head to ¼ in. thick. Round the head and the body, leaving wood for the antennae. Finish shaping the legs. Carve the antennae, leaving knobs on the ends. To prevent paint from bleeding to adjacent areas, carve grooves between the body stripes.

Suggested Colors

Body: black and yellow
Head: yellow
Facial features: black ink
Wings: antique white

Sunflower

Shown larger than actual size

GRAIN →

Pattern
(100%)
© 2001 Gary Batte

Finished Size
¼ in. thick by 2 in. diameter

Carving Notes
Draw a 2-inch circle on a ¼-inch-thick piece of wood. Draw another circle 1⅜ in. in diameter inside the outer circle. Saw out the 2-inch-diameter circle. Carve the outer ring, which will be the petals, down to ⅛ in. thick. Round the center portion to a convex shape and make small indentations to resemble seeds with a 2 mm veiner or other tool. Mark the petals and make a stop cut along each of the larger petals. Cut a ¹⁄₁₆ in. deep trough between the large petals to create an overlapping effect. Slightly round the edges of the petals.

Suggested Colors
Flower: yellow and burnt umber

Apple Samplers

Knife Only

Shown larger than actual size

Pattern
(100%)
© 2001 Gary Batte

GRAIN

Worm is
carved
separately

Finished Size

⅜ in. thick by 1⅛ in. wide by 1⅜ in. tall

Carving Notes

Round the apple and remove the surplus wood from the front of the leaf and stem. Shape the leaf and stem. Drill a ³⁄₃₂ in. hole in one side. Carve the worm separately to fit the hole.

Finished Size

½ in. thick by 1⅜ in. wide by 1⅝ in. tall

Carving Notes

Use the same procedure as above. The "bite" was cut with the band saw. The "teeth" marks were carved with a 3 mm veiner. The bite mark is left unpainted.

Suggested Colors for both projects

Apple: Napthol red light/raw umber mix

Stem: burnt umber

Leaf: Jubilee green/raw umber mix

Worm: yellow and black

GRAIN

Pattern
(100%)
© 2001 Gary Batte

Tommy Tomato

Shown larger than actual size

Pattern
(100%)
© 2001 Gary Batte

Finished Size

½ in. thick by 2¹⁄₁₆ in. wide by 1⅜ in. tall

Carving Notes

Carve the stem back to about ⅛ in. thick. Carve around the nose with a veiner and a gouge. Round the nose and the rest of the tomato. Carve around the stem details with a 3 mm gouge to minimize splitting. Refer to the *Santa Mouse* project on page 38 for instructions on carving the eyes.

Suggested Colors

Tomato skin: orange/Napthol red light mix
Stem: Hunter green/raw umber mix
Eyes: white and black
Mouth: black ink

Ribbit

Shown larger than actual size

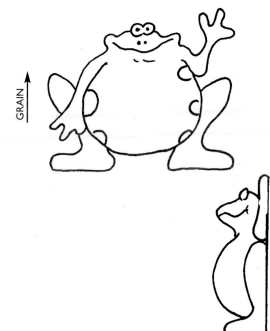

Pattern
(100%)
© 2001 Gary Batte

Finished Size

½ in. thick by 2³⁄₁₆ in. wide by 1¹³⁄₁₆ in. tall

Carving Notes

Mark a centerline down the front of the piece. Carve the surplus wood from the front of each leg; leave wood for the feet and extra thickness for the right front foot and leg. Carve surplus wood from the front side of each foot, angling the foot toward the rear.

Carve a groove beneath the chin with a ³⁄₁₆ in. veiner to separate the chin from the belly. Begin rounding the belly. Using a 3 mm veiner, carve wood from the eyes and above the nose; then slightly round the mouth area.

Use a 3 mm veiner to separate the toes and round the legs and feet. Complete rounding the belly. Round the eyeballs with the tip of a knife or small skew chisel.

Suggested Colors

Body: jubilee green/raw umber mix
Spots: hunter green
Eyes: white with black dots

Man In the Moon

Shown larger than actual size

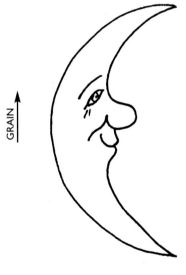

Pattern
(100%)
© 2001 Gary Batte

GRAIN

Finished Size
⅔ in. thick by 1½ in. wide by 2⅝ in. tall

Carving Notes

Round the front and slightly round the "points." Make a stop cut along the nostril and smile lines with a knife. Round the nose and the smile line.

Carve the eye socket with a no. 9, 6 mm gouge. Refer to the *Uncle Sam* project on page 5 to carve the eye.

Carve the mouth. Make a shallow cut with a gouge just below the lower lip.

Suggested Colors
Moon: yellow
Eye: white and black with a white dot for highlight
Brow: black ink

Speed-O

Shown larger than actual size

Pattern
(100%)
© 2001 Gary Batte

GRAIN

Finished Size
¼ in. thick by 2¼ in. wide by 1⅝ in. tall

Carving Notes
Carve a small amount of wood from just above the lower edge of the shell with a no. 9, 6 mm gouge to create a flair effect. Round the rest of the shell. Carve the legs, the tail and the neck to about a ⅛ in. thickness and round. Round the head.

Suggested Colors
Turtle: Jubilee green/raw umber mix (darker areas have more raw umber)
Eyes: white with black dot
Facial features: black ink

Toadstool

Shown larger than actual size

Finished Size

½ in. thick by 1¾ in. wide by 1¾ in. tall

Carving Notes

Round the stem to ¼ in. thick. Round the top, flaring the lower edge. Round the edges.

Suggested Colors

Stem: burnt umber

Cap: antique white with red iron oxide spots

GRAIN

Pattern
(100%)

© 2001 Gary Batte

Fun Flower

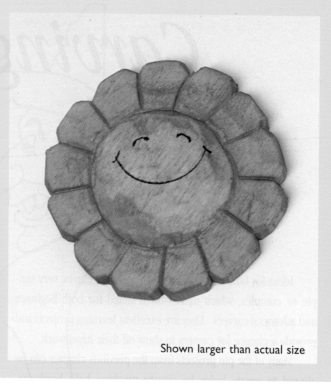

Shown larger than actual size

GRAIN →

Pattern
(100%)
© 2001 Gary Batte

Finished Size
¼ in. thick by 1⅞ in. diameter

Carving Notes
Carve the petals down to ¼ in. thick and round the center of the flower. Carve divisions between the petals with a knife and a v-tool.

Suggested Colors
Petals: violet

Center: dark brown

Facial features: black ink

Winking Santa

Shown larger than actual size

Finished Size

1⅛ in. thick by 1⅛ in. wide by 3 in. tall

Carving Notes

Bandsaw the front view and mark the side view. Carve the surplus from above the nose. Mark a center line on the nose.

Use a veiner to carve the surplus wood from the front of the cap tassel and round the edge of the beard adjacent to the cheeks. Round the cap, stopping at the tassel. Round the head and beard and tassel.

Mark the nose and mustache. Carve around the nose with a small veiner, leaving the left wing slightly higher than the right. Shape the nose and carve the right eye socket. The right eye brow is arched higher than the left. Leave wood for the brow to sag downward and for the left cheek to be pulled upward under the eye.

Carve the mustache and round the mouth area. Carve the lips, teeth and tongue. A small skew chisel is good for rounding and smoothing the tongue. Carve a groove below the lower lip with a gouge. Refer to the *Cowpoke Bolo* project on page 56 for techniques on carving the eyes, brows and hair. Wrinkles around the eyes and bridge of the nose are important. Use a sharp knife tip or v-tool to carve these.

Suggested Colors

Cap : Napthol red light/raw umber mix with white trim
Eye: white with cobalt blue/raw umber mix for the iris, black ink
Face: flesh tone with Vermilion red watercolor blended on the
    cheeks, nose, lips and beneath eyes
Tongue: very thin Napthol red light

GRAIN

Pattern
(100%)
© 2001 Gary Batte

Barfy Buzzard

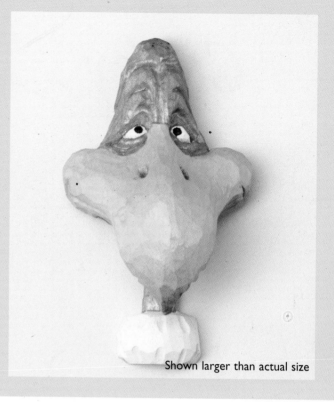

Shown larger than actual size

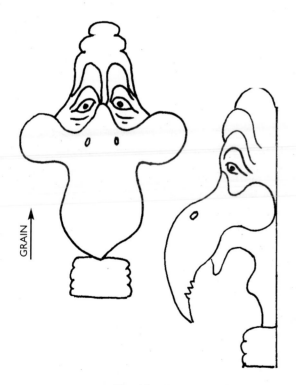

Pattern
(100%)
© 2001 Gary Batte

Finished Size
1¼ in. thick by 1⅞ in. wide by 3 in. tall

Carving Notes

Band saw the side and front views. Round the head and shape the beak. Carve the eye sockets; then carve the eyes, using the same basic procedure described in the *Cowpoke Bolo* project on page 56. Carve the wrinkles around the head. Carve the neck and the neck feathers.

Suggested Colors

Head and neck: Napthol red light/raw umber mix
Whiskers on top of head: woodburned
Eyes: white with black ink
Beak: Yellow oxide/raw umber mix with black blended on the tip
Neck feathers: white

Chapter Three

Corky Clown

Finished Size

Head dimensions: 1⅛ in. thick by 2⅜ in. wide by 2⅝ in. tall

Feet dimensions: ⅝ in. thick by 1⅛ in. wide by 2⅛ in. long

Carving Notes

Head: Band saw, then mark a square for the nose. Carve wood from around the square to the depth of the nose; allow for the lip to curve outward beneath the nose. Round the square to the point of attachment. This is best accomplished by first carving the corners off the square; then rounding the edges.

Round the hat crown and brim. Carve the surplus wood from around the face and back to the hair line. Round the face, leaving a mound for the mouth area. Carve the mouth and the bow tie. Refer to the *Cowpoke Bolo* on page 56 project for instructions on carving the eyes. Use a 6 mm gouge to carve the hair texture.

Feet: Round the toe and shape the heel and tongue, leaving wood for the strings. Remove wood from around and between the strings and carve the knot. Remove wood from inside the shoe with a small gouge to about a ³⁄₁₆ in. depth.

Pattern
(100%)

© 2001 Gary Batte

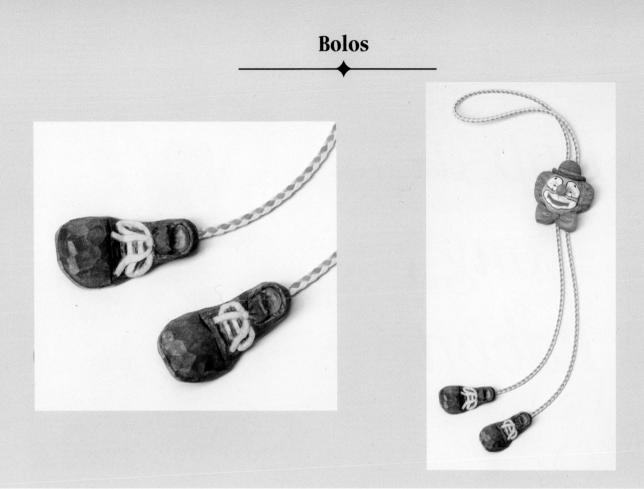

Carve the sole and heel separations with a v-tool. Drill a ⅛ in. by ½ in. hole in the back of the heel to accommodate the bolo rope.

Suggested Colors

Face: medium flesh with white around eyes and mouth; outline white with black ink

Mouth and nose: Napthol red light

Eyes: white, cobalt blue, black; accent above eyes with cobalt blue

Hair: burnt sienna

Hat: cobalt blue, violet

Tie: Jubilee green

Shoes: Dioxazine purple, yellow, raw umber

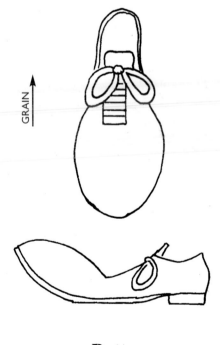

GRAIN

¹⁄8 hole

Pattern
(100%)
© 2001 Gary Batte

Hop-a-Long Rabbit

Shown larger than actual size

Finished Size

¾ in. thick by 2⅛ in. wide by 3 in. tall.

Carving Notes

Remove wood from above the nose to the top of the carving to 9/16 in. thick. Carve any excess from between the ears, the hat brim and crown. Now remove excess from in front of the ears and the crown. Slope the brim from the front to the back and round the crown.

Carve away the excess below the brim and across the snout. Round the nose, snout and head. Carve the eyes. With a 5 mm veiner, carve the surplus from each side of the bandanna, leaving wood for the front paws and legs. Shape the paws, legs and tummy. Complete the bandanna.

Carve the ears and remove the excess wood from the surface of the brim. Carve the mouth, leaving wood for the teeth and tongue. Round the toes and carve the separations with a v-tool.

Suggested Colors

Hat: black with raw umber band
Body: burnt umber
Inside of ears: dark flesh
Bandanna: Napthol red light/raw umber mix, use toothpick for white dots
Whiskers: woodburned

Pattern
(100%)
© 2001 Gary Batte

GRAIN

Home Sweet Home

Shown larger than actual size

Pattern
(100%)
© 2001 Gary Batte

GRAIN

Finished Size

½ in. thick by 2 in. wide by 2⅞ in. tall

Carving Notes

Carve the surplus wood from the side of the bird house, angling from the front to the back. Leave wood for the flower. Carve each flower petal by pressing the end of a ⅛ in. veiner straight into the wood, then removing wood from around the indentation.

Carve the roof in the same manner as the side, leaving wood for the bird. Carve the front, angling it slightly toward the right and back. Carve the perch at an angle, leaving it solidly attached its entire length. Carve the hole by making a 1/16 in. stop cut around the edge; then removing the wood inside. Trim the roofline to overhang about 1/16 in.

Round the bird's head and carve the beak. Shape the tail feathers and the wings. Carve the feather separations. Round the body.

Suggested Colors

House: burnt umber
Roof: hunter green/raw umber roof
Flower: hunter green, sweetheart blush and raw umber
Bird: Denim blue, yellow

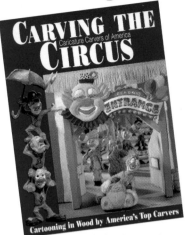
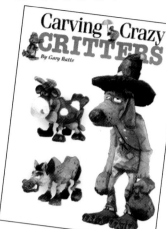

Made in the USA
Charleston, SC
26 July 2016

Network for Endangered Sea Turtles (N.E.S.T)

The Outer Banks of North Carolina is one of the northernmost ranges for sea turtles. Sea turtles are air-breathing reptiles. Sea turtles visit the Outer Banks during early-to mid-summer to lay eggs. Those eggs hatch 55-80 days after they are laid. It is estimated that only 1 sea turtle hatchling in 1,000 survives to maturity, which is approximately 18 years old.

Weighing 250-400 pounds, adult Loggerheads can grow to more than three feet in length. Adult Leatherback sea turtles can reach the size of a VW bug!

Report all nesting turtles, turtle crawls, stranded/dead turtles or hatching events on the Outer Banks to the N.E.S.T hotline 252-441-8622.

Workman Publishing featured Beau, who passed away in March 2015, in the 2016 365 dogs calendar. He was rescued from a puppy mill when 18 months old and lived to be nearly 15 years old.

(Left to right) Petunia, Potter, Beemer, Lexi, Bogie, Jack, (below bench). Camera shy, Hannah.

All 7 dogs are rescues. They are great dogs that bring smiles to people wherever they go. Beemer and Lexi, are therapy dogs. They run freely on the beaches in the Outer Banks unleashed and in parks in New Jersey.

Please consider adopting your next best friend. Internet sale of puppies and pet store puppies are mostly from commercial puppy mills. These mills are cruel breeding establishments that care nothing about the dog's well-being and the dogs are bred over and over for profit. Many puppies from puppy mills have health issues.

ABOUT THE AUTHOR

Janice Kingsbury

Janice is a school psychologist and teacher. She grew up in New Jersey and lives there part of the time, but spends a great deal of her time at her home in Duck, North Carolina. It is on the beaches of Duck that she was inspired to write her children's books. Her other books include Lexi Goes on Vacation to the Outer Banks and Chihuahuas Like Cheese. Her late Shetland sheepdog dog, Beau, won a place as Calendar dog in 365 Dogs 2016 calendar published by Workman's Publishing. She has been featured in the Philadelphia Inquirer, Burlington County Times, and Chestnut Hill Local.

Janice has fostered and rescued more than 50 neglected-abused dogs and has worked with hundreds of other dogs. Her current brood, with the passing of Beau, is 7. She originally wrote her books to increase awareness of animal rescue. Her books are fun and often have important life lessons, which children will enjoy. Adults also enjoy her books.

Petunia made a full recovery and the dogs continue to enjoy the beach. Ms. J takes the dogs for walks in the neighborhood if the beach is stormy or red flags are posted.

Bogie never swam again, but will prance into the water up to his knees. He holds his head a little higher, sings a little louder, and has started to trim down from all his walks. He's one of the pack and he's quite happy with himself these days.

Ms. J carries her phone for emergencies only. She enjoys her four-legged friends and all the great things to see at the beach because that's what matters most in life.

Around September, Ms. J and the dogs combed the beach looking for the hatchlings near the place the big turtle had nested, hoping some had survived. They also scanned the waters for evidence of the turtle, the mystical creature that had saved Petunia.

They never again saw the turtle or the babies.

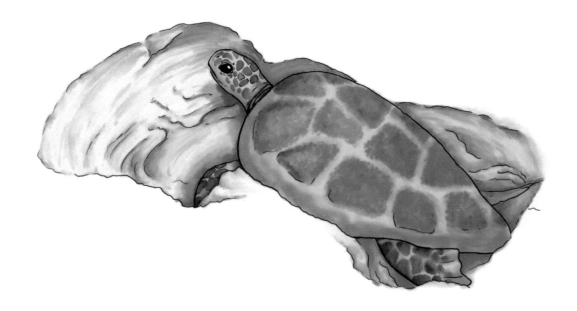

The huge turtle crawled to a sandy area and made a nest about two feet deep. There she deposited her eggs and just as quickly did an about-face and returned to the sea, leaving a huge turtle crawl in the sand to mark her journey. Ms. J stared after this marvelous creature that had saved Petunia. Ms. J said a silent prayer of thank you and hoped the baby turtles would survive.

There clinging to the turtle's back, holding on for all her life, was Petunia, safe and sound. Petunia was a little wobbly from her battle in the water. She coughed and spit out the salt water for several minutes and she was shivering. Beemer had made his way out of the water and was by Ms. J's side to check on Petunia. Ms. J cried tears as she took Petunia home for a warm blanket and chicken broth.

AND what she saw took her breath away. Huge feet and head, a creature the size of a small Volkswagen bug was swimming with her, toward shore. Ms. J came up for air. The turtle was so big and strong, that it easily swam through the current until the big shell glided onto the beach.

Almost there, another few feet, Ms. J chanted. She lunged for Petunia's collar. As she grabbed she could feel the buckle on the collar slip away as a wave crashed over them both, sending Ms. J in a tumble under the water. She quickly righted herself, spitting out salt water. But when she came up she couldn't spot the black dog in the dark, unforgiving sea. With tears mixed with blood streaming down her cheeks, Ms. J dove underneath the waves to search for her.

Losing no time, Ms. J put Bogie in her backpack and used all her strength to push through the strong currents. "I'm coming Petunia, I'm coming," she yelled. The sky was dark now with another storm coming. The wind was blowing her hair in her face. "Petunia," she screamed!

As she scooped Bogie into her arms, Ms. J let out a scream. Petunia, who had followed Beemer into the surf, had been pulled out into deep water by the strong currents. She was struggling against the rip current as it whirled her round and round in circles. Her big ears stood straight up and she could barely keep her head above water.

Bogie's bark could barely be heard against the wind and sound of waves. Ms. J was busy checking pictures for the perfect post until something in the water got her attention.

Bogie was coming toward her, paddling his little legs for all he was worth. Then with head raised, he let out his loudest, ear piercing Chihuahua sound ever. It sounded croaky, like a foghorn, but loud.

Ms. J thought the beach was even more beautiful today after the storm. The waves were angry and strong. The sky was grayer but had slashes of pink and silver. The pier was covered with a film of smoky mist and foggy clouds. Maybe a picture with her cell and then she would post it on Facebook.

Bogie, who stood by Ms. J, ran quickly away to avoid a big wave. Ms. J stood knee deep in the water taking pictures and checking email messages.

Even the birds were happy for a break in the weather to look for food. There were crowds of cormorants, sanderlings and plovers on the beach. The dogs came alive as they chased the birds back and forth through the rough surf. Petunia gave up looking for crabs and followed Beemer as she often did. Up and down the beach they ran.

Then, after a week of wind and rain, the sky began to clear. "C'mon said Ms. J. We're going to the beach." It was windy and the red flags were flying on the beach meaning "caution," the ocean is rough. The high waves reached out with their white, curling foam fingers, crashing loudly against the banks and carving out big cliffs in the sand. In some places, there was little land left to walk, but everyone did their best, happy to be out.

The dogs were stuck in the house so long that tempers were flaring. Teeth were bared and food stolen from other's bowls at dinnertime. Lexi, the biggest dog, pretended to herd sheep in the living room. He would run in circles, bark and dip over and over until he got on Bogie's last nerve. When Bogie couldn't take any more he tried to mark his little spot and lifted his leg on the sofa. Lexi sniffed the spot, but it didn't make him stop.

By midsummer the heat was unbearable and so the cool rain was, at first, a welcome relief. But day after day it rained and gusts of wind blew. Each day Ms. J woke to the patter of raindrops and sound of the wind blowing the wind chimes. The street was empty and even Mr. Mark couldn't be seen standing by his garage. His door had been down for days.

After that day, Bogie would prance proudly into the surf up to his knees and often be rewarded with a treat. Once again, he was part of the pack and he could do what the others did without feeling angry. He looked at Ms. J lovingly and didn't lift his leg in the house anymore.

One day at the sound beach, the tide was very low and there was a little sand island about 10 feet from the shore. Ms. J put her chair there and was enjoying the sun. Bogie was alone on the bank as usual. Tired of being left by himself, Bogie made a decision. He took a deep breath and plunged his little feet in the water. As quickly as he could, he waded to the little spot of sand. Then he looked up at Ms. J with his big brown eyes. "I'm SO PROUD OF YOU, BOGIE," said Ms. J excitedly. "I know you were afraid." And Bogie felt proud too.

On some days, Ms. J would take the dogs to the Currituck sound instead of the beach. It was cooler there and the dogs could swim and chase birds. Beemer, the Border Collie, would have so much fun chasing the birds, that he would swim out near the boats and could barely be seen. Ms. J would have to blow the whistle to call him.

Petunia tried to follow Beemer, but swimming was new to her and she would tire more easily and have to turn back to shore.

Bogie stood alone on the shore watching the other dogs swim and have fun chasing Frisbees. He wanted to be part of the fun, but he was so afraid of the water!

Ms. J had her mind made up and put Bogie gently into the foaming surf. The water covered his ankles. Then she splashed a little water over his back. Bogie gave Ms. J his meanest look ever. Then he gave her the GRRRR sound, curled his lip and ground his teeth. Even so, Ms. J gave him a dog treat to reward him.

Petunia, who was part Chihuahua, but mostly rat terrier, loved the water and seemed to have no fear at all. Bogie thought this made him look bad. Petunia followed Beemer into the surf as he chased birds and sometimes body surfed the waves.

It was a hot day in July, and all of the dogs were cooling off in the water when Bogie heard Ms. J call him. "Bogie, you have to go in the water and get cool! It's time you got used to it!"

NO! NO! CHIHUAHUAS HATE THE WATER!!

Bogie scurried to the other side of the beach. He had not put one foot in the water, EVER. At high tide, he would walk all by himself at the top of the bank where he could stay dry. The loud crashing sounds of the waves frightened him too.

It wasn't fair that Bogie didn't get a break. The other dogs were bigger and Petunia was young and muscular. They didn't get as tired as Bogie.

The next day when Ms. J called the dogs to go out, Bogie pretended not to hear and hid under the covers. "C'mon Bogie," Ms. J said. "You can't stay home." Bogie started wiggling his body and grinding his teeth as he sometimes did when Ms. J wasn't listening to him but, Ms. J picked him up and onto the beach they went.

As it became hotter, Bogie started to become cranky. He couldn't keep up. He walked, he sat for pets and pictures, but he was so hot and tired when he got home one day, he just wanted to go to bed. Of all things, Petunia was in his bed. He gave her his best GRRRRRR.... sound, but Petunia just rolled over and Bogie had to nap on the big bed with Jack, who snored.

Bogie was a favorite and he would roll over for belly rubs. Then he would race to catch up with the others, but his legs were short and the sand was hot on his feet. Ms. J wouldn't pick him up, though he wiggled and showed his teeth. "No Bogie," she said. "You can do it!"

Every day, Ms. J and the dogs would walk on the beach to the Pier a mile away. People would stop them to chat and play with the dogs. People were very friendly and sometimes the walk would take hours.

As summer approached the weather became hotter than usual. The beaches were crowded with vacationers. Mr. Mark, when not napping, spent much of his time observing the summer crowds. "There are so many great things to see," he said. "I saw dolphins today and a great school of fish. I saw the sunrise this morning and it was beautiful." It puzzled him that vacationers spent so much time staring at their cell phones while at the beach. Mr. Mark swore he'd never own one.

Then there was the red dog that lay on the beach, dropping her ball over and over into the surf and watching it come back. Someone always rescued the ball before it washed away. Bogie had heard a rumor that the red dog ate only salad for dinner at the family restaurant, the Salad Bowl, in Kitty Hawk. He was quite trim, unlike Bogie, who had a thick middle.

At the beach, Bogie saw his friends from last year. There were the neighbors, Bea, and Ron, with their dog, Bella, and Mr. Mark, who stood by his mysterious garage by the beach to greet all of the dogs. Mr. Mark nicknamed Bella, Sideways, because she would run sideways to greet him and get a treat.

He couldn't wait to go to the beach house in Duck, North Carolina. He would nap in the cozy, cushioned chair on the deck and bathe in the warm sun. Ms. J packed Bogie's bed and blanket and lots of treats. They stopped for fresh donuts at Duck Donuts. Yes, and candy at the Sugar Shack and kites at Kitty Hawk Kites. Then onto Kellogg Hardware for beach chairs and umbrellas. One more stop at Duck Post office to mail cards and they were on their way. It promised to be a great summer!

Bogie loved Ms. J and was excited when the family packed up for the beach that spring. It had been a long cold winter and Boogie had to walk in the snow with the other dogs. Sometimes his little toes became pink from the cold, and Ms. Mary, his friend from the dog park, would pick him up and carry him.

Bogie learned how to get along with all the dogs in the house, and quickly became one of the pack even though he was the smallest of them all. He learned how to sing, chew bully sticks and go for long walks. He even learned how to get cheese, his favorite treat.

At night Bogie would sniffle when he thought no one could hear him. But finally, one day a nice lady came for him and after a long journey he ended up at an adoption event at Pet Smart. It was here he met his foster mom, Ms. J, who decided to keep the little guy. He moved in with the family in the north but spent the summers in the south in Duck, North Carolina, on the Outer Banks.

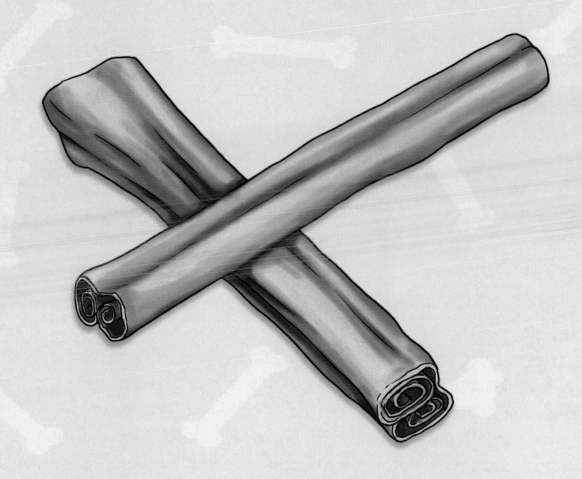

Bogie, the Chihuahua, has been through a lot in his short life. His history is uncertain, but he found himself in a shelter in South Carolina. It was not a great place for any dog, let alone a Chihuahua. He was put in a cell with other dogs that tried to eat his food. He didn't have a Chihuahua blanket or bed and was often cold. Nor did he have friends with whom to snuggle. He was sad and lonely.

SAVING PETUNIA

JANICE WILLS KINGSBURY

What abstract noun is this?

Concrete Collages

Identifying concrete and abstract nouns

For an out-of-this-world way to teach concrete and abstract nouns, write the words shown on chart paper. After discussing the words' meanings, ask, "Can you see, taste, hear, smell, or touch these nouns?" Explain that these are *abstract nouns:* words that name ideas, feelings, emotions, or qualities. Further explain that *concrete nouns* name things that can be seen, touched, tasted, heard, or smelled. Challenge students to name a concrete noun that is related to each list word (for example, *tears* or *frown* for *sadness*).

Next, have each student choose one word from the list and cut out at least six magazine pictures that illustrate its meaning. (Allow students who can't find enough pictures to draw and cut out their own illustrations.) Then have her arrange and glue the pictures collage-style on a sheet of construction paper. Finally, have each child fold an index card in half, write her abstract noun inside the resulting card, and attach the card to her picture. Ask each student to share her collage and challenge classmates to identify its abstract noun. Then post the projects on a bulletin board titled "Concrete Collages of Abstract Nouns."

anger	happiness	responsibility
beauty	joy	sadness
bravery	justice	safety
cooperation	kindness	spirit
courtesy	loneliness	strength
determination	love	talent
fear	nature	teamwork
freedom	respect	wisdom

Taking Note of Nouns

Identifying different kinds of nouns

Go on a mission to identify different types of nouns with this easy-to-do review activity. First, make a transparency of a paragraph from your current read-aloud or a novel your students are reading. Also write the different kinds of nouns on the board as shown. Review the terms with the class. Then ask students to predict how many kinds of nouns might be in the average paragraph. When all predictions have been made, project the paragraph on the overhead. One sentence at a time, have students identify and categorize the noun(s) in each sentence. When finished, count the number of nouns and compare them to the students' predictions. Follow up by having each student complete a copy of the reproducible on page 10.

singular
plural
common
proper
concrete
abstract
collective
compound

Noun Quest

Get ready for a grammar quest that will send you searching for one of the planet's most important parts of speech: the noun. Write your answers on your own paper. Use reference materials if necessary.

1. Write a noun that is very difficult for you to spell.
2. Write two nouns that can be combined to form a compound noun.
3. Write three nouns that name things you would want to have with you if you were stranded on an island.
4. List four nouns that describe you. (Careful! Don't use adjectives.)
5. List five nouns related to the book you are reading now. Write your book's title on the spaceship on this page.
6. List six nouns that are related to a science or social studies topic you are studying.
7. Write seven proper nouns that have to do with your family.
8. Write eight nouns that are found somewhere in your classroom.
9. Write nine nouns that name some of your favorite things.
10. Write ten nouns that can be found in your favorite room of your house.

Name_____ *Common and proper nouns, analogies*

Analogy Galaxy

Welcome to the Analogy Galaxy, where you can send grammar skills into orbit. How? By filling in each analogy with a common noun or a proper noun. When you're finished, circle the common nouns in yellow. Underline the proper nouns in red.

1. Nile is to river as "_____" is to movie.
2. City is to Chicago as building is to _____.
3. France is to country as _____ is to restaurant.
4. Shania Twain is to singer as _____ is to car.
5. President is to Abraham Lincoln as soda pop is to _____.
6. _____ is to state as Bermuda is to island.
7. Mars is to planet as _____ is to team.
8. Book is to _____ as holiday is to Labor Day.
9. Cereal is to _____ as apple is to Macintosh.
10. Ocean is to Atlantic as continent is to _____.

Bonus Box: Write two more analogies like the ones above on another sheet of paper. Give them to a classmate to finish.

Note to the teacher: Use "Analogy Galaxy" with "Picturing Nouns" on page 5. Each student will need red and yellow crayons or markers.

Picture-Perfect Plurals

moose
crash
butterfly
hero
deer
man
mouse
truck

life
penny
rodeo
leaf
sheep
fox
half
clock

cherry
key
candy
wolf
child
dress
foot

Part I: On your own paper, write the plural spelling of each word. Then write each plural in the shape with the matching rule.

Add *s*.

Add *es*.

Change *y* to *i* and add *es*.

Change *f* or *fe* to *v* and add *es*.

Do not change.

Change to an irregular spelling.

Part 2: Lightly color each shape. Use a ruler to divide a large sheet of construction paper into six equal-sized sections. Then cut out each shape and glue it in one section of the paper. In each section, write five other plural nouns that follow the shape's rule.

©2000 The Education Center, Inc. • *Grammar Plus!* • *Parts of Speech* • TEC2315 • Key p. 47

Note to the teacher: Use with "Rise and Sign!" on page 5. Provide each student with a copy of this page, a ruler, a 12" x 18" sheet of construction paper, crayons, scissors, glue, and fine-tipped markers or colored pencils. Let students share their posters when finished.

9

Noteworthy Nouns

Acxkhdu, from the planet Ksqopsug, loves two things: tooting his schnozzle (that's his nose) and noodling with nouns. Help him complete the chart below while he plays a planetary tune on his proboscis (that means *nose* too). Draw an X in each box that describes that noun. Each noun will have more than one X beside it when you're finished. The first word is done for you.

KINDS OF NOUNS — common	proper	concrete	abstract	collective	singular	plural	compound	
X		X				X	X	flashlights
								school
								liberty
								onions
								Eiffel Tower
								fear
								Juanita
								perfume
								Hayes Middle School
								responsibilities
								baby-sitter
								antennae
								Glenn Miller Orchestra
								family
								deer
								New York Mets
								great-grandmother
								blueberries

Bonus Box: On the back of this page or another sheet of paper, write a paragraph that describes the day Acxkhdu landed his spaceship in your backyard. Include at least five plural nouns.

Verbs

A **verb** is a word that describes action or a state of being. It is the main word in the predicate of a sentence.

- An **action verb** is a word that describes a physical or mental action.

  EXAMPLES   The coach **pointed** to the goal line.
  The coach **listened** to the quarterback's suggestion.

- A **linking verb** links the subject to a noun or adjective in the predicate of the sentence. A linking verb says that something is, was, or will be. It does not show action.

  EXAMPLES   I **will be** the speaker at tomorrow's assembly.
  She **is** the mayor of our town.
  The garbage **smells** funny.

- A **helping verb** comes before the main verb. It helps state an action or show time. A main verb can have from one to three helping verbs. The helping verbs are *am, are, be, being, been, can, could, did, do, does, had, has, have, is, may, might, must, shall, should, was, were, will, would.*

  EXAMPLES   Rita **was** smiling at her new puppy.
  Carl **has** written his story.
  I **should have** done my homework.

- The subject and verb of a sentence must agree in number.

  — A **singular verb** is used when the subject of a sentence is singular.

  EXAMPLE   Spot **likes** to chew my shoes. (**Spot** and **likes** are both singular.)

  — A **plural verb** is used when the subject of a sentence is plural.

  EXAMPLE   Some birds **eat** worms. (**Birds** and **eat** are both plural.)

- A verb is **active** if the subject of the sentence is doing the action.

> **EXAMPLE**   Birds **flew** out of the nest. (The subject **birds** is doing the action.)

- A verb is **passive** if the subject is not doing the action.

> **EXAMPLE**   A cake **was made** by Gina. (The subject cake isn't doing the action.)

- A **regular verb** ends in *ed* when stating a past action or when using a helping verb. Most verbs in English are regular.

> **EXAMPLE**   I **cook.**
> I **cooked** yesterday.
> I **have cooked.**

- An **irregular verb** does not end in *ed* when stating a past action or when using a helping verb.

> **EXAMPLES**   I **write.**
> I **wrote** yesterday.
> I **have written.**

- **Tense** is the time of a verb. The three most common verb tenses are:

— **Present tense:** states an action that is happening now or that happens regularly

> **EXAMPLES**   I **cook** dinner at 6:30 each night.
> I **like** this book.

— **Past tense:** states an action that has already happened.

> **EXAMPLE**   Tina **bought** the vase last week.

— **Future tense:** states an action that will happen in the future.

> **EXAMPLE**   Grandfather Jones **will visit** next week.

Action All Around Us

Identifying action verbs

The lion pounced!

Send students on a hunt for action verbs with an activity that also sharpens observation skills. After reviewing the definition of *action verb* (see page 11), display several magazine pictures that show people engaged in various activities. Have students identify the action(s) in each picture and suggest related action verbs. Next, have each student carry a book, a sheet of paper, and a pencil as you take the class for a brief walk around your school. Direct each child to list the actions he witnesses during the walk. When you return to the classroom, have students read aloud their lists, in the form of action verbs. Record the verbs on a sheet of chart paper titled "Action All Around Us." Challenge students to add other action verbs to the list throughout the rest of the week.

Billy sped past the house.
Aaron blew the candles out with
    all his might.
Cara dove off the high dive.
Ellie leaped high in the air.

Looking for Action

Identifying action verbs

Looking for a way to put students' verb skills into action? Ask each child to bring to school a photo of herself (one that doesn't need to be returned) engaged in some type of activity. Bring in photos for students who can't provide their own. Next, divide the class into groups. Give each group a sheet of chart paper, glue, and a marker. Direct the group to write a sentence for each of its photos on the chart paper, making sure that the sentence includes an action verb. Next, have the group glue the photos to the paper. As each group shares its poster, challenge the class to identify each sentence's action verb and then match the sentence with the correct photo.

Thinking 'bout Linking

Identifying linking verbs

Help students learn about verbs that can be both linking and action verbs with this fun activity. First, have each student tape a pencil to the back of a small paper plate. Then have her use a marker to write an *A* on one side of the plate and an *L* on the other. Next, write these sentences on the board: *Georgia <u>smelled</u> smoke. The soup <u>smelled</u> delicious.* Explain that sometimes a linking verb in one sentence can be an action verb in another. For example, *smelled* in the first sentence is an action that the subject *(Georgia)* took. In the second sentence, the subject *(soup)* doesn't do the action; instead, *smelled* links *soup* with a predicate adjective *(delicious)*.

Next, display one of the sentences shown on an overhead transparency. Ask the class to identify the verb. Then tell students to hold up their plates at your signal to indicate whether the verb is an action verb (A) or a linking verb (L). As an extension, list the linking verbs shown on the board; then have student pairs write sentences to use in another practice session.

SAMPLE SENTENCES

1. The baby grows prettier every day. *(linking)*
2. Farmer Jones grows corn and beans. *(action)*
3. My cats smell their food before eating. *(action)*
4. Roses smell so lovely. *(linking)*
5. Millie tasted the pancakes while they were hot. *(action)*
6. That cupcake tasted great! *(linking)*
7. The magician appeared on stage like magic. *(action)*
8. She appeared happy to me. *(linking)*
9. That song really did sound funny to me. *(linking)*
10. You should sound the fire alarm! *(action)*
11. She always feels the fur on Mom's coat. *(action)*
12. My cat's fur feels so soft. *(linking)*

Common linking verbs: to be, to seem, to appear, to taste, to grow, to look, to sound, to feel, to become, to smell, to remain

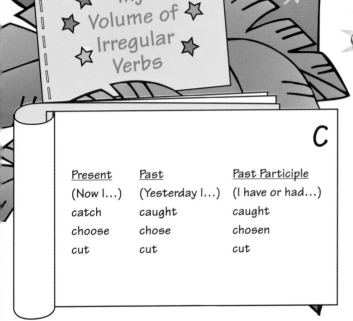

My Volume of Irregular Verbs

Present	Past	Past Participle
(Now I...)	(Yesterday I...)	(I have or had...)
catch	caught	caught
choose	chose	chosen
cut	cut	cut

C

Volumes of Irregular Verbs

Identifying irregular verbs

Track down tricky irregular verbs with a can't-be-beat project! Have each student staple 26 half sheets of notebook paper between two half sheets of construction paper. After the child adds the title shown to the cover of the resulting booklet, have him label each page with an alphabet letter and the three headings shown. Finally, challenge students to look in books and other reading material for irregular verbs to list in their dictionaries. To help, post a running list of the irregular verbs that students find. Encourage students to add to the list whenever they locate a new irregular verb.

Roll a Sentence

Skill **Identifying active and passive verbs**

All you need for this game is a pair of dice and students who like to have fun! Write each of these verbs on a separate slip of paper: *throw, draw, eat, write, drive, buy, pin, cook, wash, sing, cut, paint, kick, push, break, choose, speak, hold, hide, fly.* Place the slips in a container. Then divide the class into three teams to play this game:

1. A student from Team 1 rolls the dice, draws a slip, announces the verb, and then returns the slip to the container.
2. If the number rolled is even, the team must write a sentence using the verb (or any form of it) as an active verb. For example, if the verb is *draw* and the student rolls a six, the team might write "Kate drew the picture."
3. If the number rolled is odd, the team must use the verb as a passive verb. For example the team might write "The picture was drawn by Kate."
4. If the sentence is correct, the team scores the number of points rolled. If the sentence is incorrect, no points are scored.
5. If doubles are rolled, the team earns that number of points without having to write a sentence.
6. Play continues with Teams 2 and 3. The team with the most points at the end of the game wins.

Can't We Just Agree?

Skill **Using singular and plural verbs correctly**

For a verb game that everyone will agree on, make a copy of the bottom half of page 18. Cut out the cards. Then place the subjects in one paper bag and the verbs in another. After reviewing singular and plural verbs (see page 11), have a student pull a card from each bag and announce the resulting sentence. Without worrying about whether the sentence makes sense, ask students to decide if the subject and verb agree. If they don't agree, have the class suggest ways to change the subject or verb to make the two parts agree. Then return the cards to the bags. Continue until each student has a turn.

Tales of the Past, Present, and Future

Using verb tenses correctly

Combine a lesson on past, present, and future verb tenses with an activity that's just "write" for your next writing workshop. Divide the class into pairs and post a copy of the chart shown. Each twosome rolls a die once to select a topic and again to choose a tense. Then the pair writes a brief story using the topic and tense rolled. After students are finished, each twosome reads its story aloud. Challenge the rest of the class to identify the verbs used while you list them on the board. (Ask the pair to read the story aloud a second time if necessary.) Then have the class identify the tense used. If desired, let pairs illustrate their stories on art paper. Bind the stories and pictures in a class book titled "Tales of the Past, Present, and Future."

Roll a topic:
1—My Perfect Weekend
2—A Day With My Hero
3—My First Day as President
4—Invisible for a Day!
5—What a Weird Day at School!
6—Winning the Jackpot

Roll a tense:
1 or 6—present tense
2 or 5—past tense
3 or 4—future tense

A Poetic Part of Speech

Reviewing verb skills

Digging around for a great way to end a unit on verbs? Well, put down your shovel! Use the guide shown to cut out the letters *VERBS* from large sheets of bulletin board paper. Review verb types, forms, and tenses studied with students. Then divide the class into five groups. Challenge each group to write a poem that includes as much information about verbs as possible. When students have finished writing and proofreading their poems, give each group one of the large cutout letters and some colorful fine-tipped markers. Have the group copy its poem onto its letter. Then mount the giant display on a classroom or school hallway wall.

Cut out the black areas.

VERBS

Name_____

Animals in Action

Directions: In each blank, write an action verb that begins with the same letter as the sentence's animal. Then finish the sentence using at least one more word that begins with that letter. The first one is done for you. Hint: A sentence can be silly as long as it includes an action verb.

Dear, you <u>dance</u> divinely!

A. An aardvark _asked an ant for his address._____.

B. A barking baboon _____.

C. A cool cat _____.

D. The dirty dog _____.

E. Each elephant _____.

F. The friendly frog _____.

G. Gorillas _____.

H. A happy hippo _____.

I. The iguana _____.

J. A jackrabbit _____.

K. Kiki's kangaroo _____.

L. One lanky leopard _____.

M. Many monkeys _____.

N. The nine newts _____.

O. Only the octopus _____.

P. Prissy peacocks _____.

Q. Quite impressive! Keep going!

R. Red roosters _____.

S. Seven swans _____.

T. The timid turtles _____.

U. Uh-oh! The unicorns _____.

V. The vultures _____.

W. A wildebeest _____.

X. X marks the spot where you are almost finished!

Y. Yellow yaks _____.

Z. Zany zebras _____.

Bonus Box: On the back of this sheet or on your own paper, write five more animal sentence starters like the ones above. Give your paper to a classmate so he or she can finish the starters using action verbs.

Help Yourself to Helping Verbs!

A *helping verb* comes before the main verb. It helps state an action or show time. Look at the helping verbs in the V to the right. Use them to fill in the puzzle below.

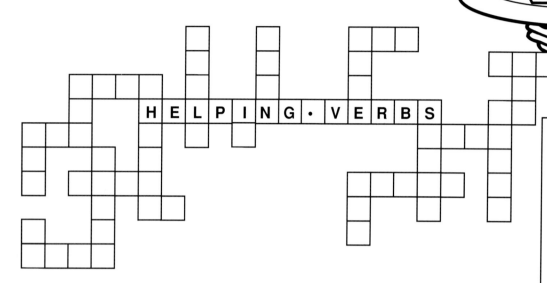

H E L P I N G · V E R B S

Bonus Box: Write several sentences about your favorite restaurant. Include at least ten different helping verbs in the sentences. Circle each helping verb and underline each main verb.

SUBJECT	SUBJECT	VERB
Three hungry lions	A huge hippo	can sing
SUBJECT The tourist guides	**SUBJECT** The old truck	**VERB** will be eating
SUBJECT The tired men	**SUBJECT** Mr. Mutley	**VERB** am running
SUBJECT Karen and Diane	**SUBJECT** My grandmother	**VERB** is painting
SUBJECT They	**VERB** ran	**VERB** has walked
SUBJECT Our friends	**VERB** climbed	**VERB** writes
SUBJECT The expedition	**VERB** was laughing	**VERB** have ridden
SUBJECT The silly monkey	**VERB** walk	**VERB** were talking

Safari Search

Directions: Read the information in the box below. Then help Wrong Way Willie find his way back to the tour group by filling in the missing verb forms in the blanks below.

The past tense of a **regular verb** is formed by adding *ed* to the verb:
    Today I walk.   Yesterday I walked.
The past participle of a regular verb (the part that's used with the helping verbs *has, have,* or *had)* is also formed by adding *ed.*
    I have walked.   She has walked.   We had walked.
The past tense and past participle of an **irregular verb** is not formed by adding *ed.*
    Today I drive.   Yesterday I drove.   I have driven.

START

1. Today I begin.
Yesterday I _____ .
I have _____ .

2. Today I say.
Yesterday I _____ .
I have _____ .

3. Today I _____ .
Yesterday I cleaned.
I have _____ .

4. Today I _____ .
Yesterday I laughed.
I have _____ .

5. Today I sing.
Yesterday I _____ .
I have _____ .

10. Today I jump.
Yesterday I _____ .
I have _____ .

9. Today I _____ .
Yesterday I wrote.
I have _____ .

8. Today I weave.
Yesterday I _____ .
I have _____ .

7. Today I take.
Yesterday I _____ .
I have _____ .

6. Today I _____ .
Yesterday I hid.
I have _____ .

11. Today I listen.
Yesterday I _____ .
I have _____ .

12. Today I catch.
Yesterday I _____ .
I have _____ .

13. Today I _____ .
Yesterday I yelled.
I have _____ .

14. Today I yawn.
Yesterday I _____ .
I have _____ .

15. Today I choose.
Yesterday I _____ .
I have _____ .

FINISH

20. Today I _____ .
Yesterday I flew.
I have _____ .

19. Today I watch.
Yesterday I _____ .
I have _____ .

18. Today I spring.
Yesterday I _____ .
I have _____ .

17. Today I bring.
Yesterday I _____ .
I have _____ .

16. Today I spin.
Yesterday I _____ .
I have _____ .

Note to the teacher: If desired, have each student use a crayon or marker to outline each box above that includes an irregular verb.

Versatile Verbs!

Complete _____ of these projects by this date: _____.

Verbs That Help Out

Cut out five comic strips from a newspaper and glue them to a sheet of construction paper. On notebook paper, write a sentence about each comic that includes at least one of these helping verbs: *am, are, is, was, were, be, being, been, do, does, did, have, has, had, may, must, might, can, could, would, should, shall, will.* Underline the helping verb(s) once. Underline the main verb twice. Staple your sentences to your comics.

In Other Words

Use a thesaurus to find four synonyms for each of the verbs listed below. Be sure your synonyms are all verbs.

| take | teach | tell |
| talk | think | tug |

One Word, Two Jobs

Many words can be both a noun and a verb, depending on how they are used. For example:
She caught a huge fish. (*Fish* is a noun.)
We will fish in the lake. (*Fish* is the main verb.)
List ten other words that can be both a noun and a verb. For each word, write a pair of sentences like the two examples above.

Taking Verbs "Cereal-ly"

All you need for this project is a pencil, an empty cereal box and three colored pencils: blue, red, and green. Write ten sentences about information that is on your box. Follow these guidelines.
• Three sentences must include action verbs.
• Three sentences must include helping verbs.
• Three sentences must include linking verbs.
Underline each verb in your sentences using colored pencils and this code:
blue = action verb, red = helping verb, green = linking verb.

The Grammar Gazette

Verbs Make Headlines!

Look through an old newspaper or magazine to find ten headlines that include verbs. Cut out each headline and glue it to a sheet of construction paper. Circle the verb with a marker.

Note to the teacher: Fill in the blanks at the top of the page before making student copies. If desired, use the activities on this page as group classwork assignments instead of as projects for individual students.

Pronouns

A pronoun is a word that is used in place of a noun.

- **Personal pronouns** include subject pronouns, object pronouns, and possessive pronouns.

  — A **subject pronoun** is used as the subject of a sentence. Subject pronouns are *I, you, he, she, it, we,* and *they*.

  EXAMPLE   **We** were right on time for the party.

  — An **object pronoun** is used after an action verb or as the object of a prepositional phrase. Object pronouns include *me, you, him, her, it, us,* and *them*.

  EXAMPLES   **He** always calls me. (comes after action verb *calls*)
  Mary waved to **him**. (object of prepositional phrase *to him*)

  — A **possessive pronoun** takes the place of a possessive noun. Possessive pronouns include *my, mine, your, yours, his, her, hers, its, our, ours, their,* and *theirs*.

  EXAMPLE   **Her** shirt is dirtier than **mine**.

- **Singular pronouns** refer to a single person or thing. They include *I, me, my, mine, he, she, him, her, his, hers, it, its,* and *you*. Use a singular pronoun with a singular verb.

- **Plural pronouns** refer to more than one person or thing. They are *we, us, our, ours, they, them, their, theirs,* and *you*.

- Pronouns must **agree** in number with the words they replace.

  EXAMPLES   Al's **yard** looked great after **it** was mowed. (Singular *it* replaces singular *yard*.)
  Millie hung the **pictures** after **they** were dry. (Plural *they* replaces plural *pictures*.)

- Five other kinds of pronouns are:

— **Demonstrative pronouns** point out nouns without naming them. They include *this, that, these,* and *those.*

> **EXAMPLE**   **That** is a great present!

— **Interrogative pronouns** ask questions. They include *what, which, who, whom,* and *whose.*

> **EXAMPLES**   **Which** can I take with me?
> I want to know **who** said that!

— **Indefinite pronouns** refer to nouns in a general way without naming the words they replace. They include *all, another, any, anybody, anyone, anything, both, each, either, everybody, everyone, everything, few, many, most, much, neither, nobody, none, no one, nothing, one, other, others, several, some, somebody, someone,* and *something.*

> **EXAMPLE**   **Everything** is packed in the car.

— **Intensive pronouns** emphasize the words they refer to. They include *myself, himself, herself, yourself, itself, themselves, yourselves,* and *ourselves.*

> **EXAMPLE**   Ted **himself** was impressed with his story.

— **Reflexive pronouns** refer back to the subject of a sentence. The same pronouns that are intensive pronouns are also reflexive.

> **EXAMPLE**   Lucy surprised even **herself.**

Prowling for Pronouns

Skill **Identifying and categorizing personal pronouns by case**

Send students on the prowl for personal pronouns with this activity! Post the chart shown. After reviewing personal pronouns with students (see page 21), have each child take out the same book (a novel the class is reading or a basal reader). Then divide the class into groups. Challenge each group to locate a page that appears to have a large number of pronouns. After all members agree on the page, direct the group to list and count the pronouns. When time is up, have each group share its list as you write the words on the board. If desired, award a small treat or class privilege to the team that located the most pronouns. Extend the activity by having each group categorize its words according to whether they are subject, object, or possessive pronouns. Then have the group graph its data.

Personal Pronoun Cases

Subject Pronouns: I, you, he, she, it, we, they
Object Pronouns: me, you, him, her, it, us, them
Possessive Pronouns: my, mine, your, yours, his, her, hers, its, our, ours, their, theirs

Pronoun Toss

Skill **Using subject and object pronouns correctly**

They discovered...

Here's a gem of a game to help students use pronouns correctly! Write the subject and object pronouns shown above on the board. Then divide the class into two teams: Subject and Object. Line up the teams so that they face each other. Give a foam ball to the first Subject player. Direct her to choose a subject pronoun and use it in a simple sentence, such as "<u>She</u> ran." Then have her toss the ball to an Object player. That student adds a phrase containing an object pronoun to the sentence, such as "to <u>them</u>." The Object player then tosses the ball to another Subject player, who starts the process again. As students play, jot down five of their sentences.

After each child has had a turn, write the five sentences on the board. Then challenge the class to replace each pronoun with a noun (or noun phrase), such as "<u>Mrs. Waters</u> ran to <u>her children</u>."

Picturing Pronouns

Understanding different uses of personal pronouns

Personal pronouns can replace nouns in different ways. To help students understand some of the uses for personal pronouns, review the chart shown. Then give each pair of students scissors and some old magazines. Direct each twosome to cut out an interesting picture that shows action. Then have the pair write a short story about the picture that includes at least one of each pronoun use listed on the chart. Instruct students to underline each pronoun. Then have pairs swap papers and check each story to make sure it includes one example of each pronoun use. Have the pairs return the stories to their owners for corrections. Then post the corrected stories and pictures on a bulletin board titled "Picturing Pronouns!"

Use Personal Pronouns to:

- **Replace a subject:** Ann ate cake. <u>She</u> ate cake.
- **Replace a predicate noun:** My mother is Deb. My mother is <u>she</u>.
- **Replace a direct or an indirect object:** He hit the ball. He hit <u>it</u>. (direct object)
  I baked Bill a cake. I baked <u>him</u> a cake. (indirect object)
- **Replace the object of a preposition:** Kay sat beside her cousins. Kay sat beside <u>them</u>.
- **Show possession:** These glasses belong to Pat. These glasses belong to <u>her</u>.

Pronouns-in-a-Box

Identifying singular and plural pronouns

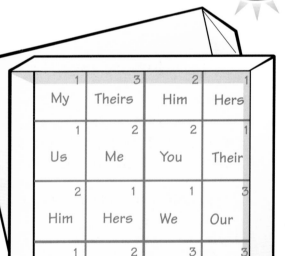

1 My	3 Theirs	2 Him	1 Hers
1 Us	2 Me	2 You	1 Their
2 Him	1 Hers	1 We	3 Our
1 I	2 He	3 Mine	3 She
1 It	3 Them	2 Its	2 His

Turn a box and a paper clip into an exciting game involving singular and plural pronouns! Draw a 4 x 5 grid in the bottom of a large gift box. In each block, write a singular or plural pronoun and a number 1–3 as shown. Then place a paper clip in the box and add the lid. The next morning have students look for pronouns throughout the day on classroom and school walls or in reading material. Direct each child to write down each sentence he spots that includes a pronoun and note whether it is singular or plural. Provide time for students to tally the number of times they spotted each pronoun. Then discuss students' findings.

Next, divide the class into two teams. In turn, a player shakes the box, sets it on his desktop, and removes the lid. Then he multiplies the number in the block containing the paper clip by the number of times he spotted that block's pronoun. The total is added to his team's score. Play until each student has a turn. Declare the team with the most points the winner.

Let's Get Personal!

Skill Understanding first-, second-, and third-person pronouns

Personal Pronouns
First Person (the person who is speaking): I, we, me, us, my, mine, our, ours
Second Person (the person spoken to): you, your, yours
Third Person (the person or thing being spoken about): he, she, it, his, her, hers, its, him, her, it, they, them, their, theirs.

Personalize a pronouns lesson with this activity on first-, second-, and third-person pronouns. Write each pronoun shown on a separate slip of paper. Put the slips into a bag. Next, divide the class into pairs. Each pair draws two slips, writes the words at the top of an index card, and returns the slips to the bag. Then the pair writes a sentence using the two words correctly. On the back of the card, the twosome writes a sentence that replaces the pronouns with underlined nouns as shown.

After collecting the cards, divide the class into two teams. Give a player from Team 1 a card. Have her copy the nouns sentence on the board. Then challenge Team 2 to guess the pronouns that the nouns replaced. Award Team 2 one point for each correct pronoun and an extra point for correctly stating whether it is first, second, or third person. Continue until all cards have been played. Then declare the team with more points the winner.

her, it
The teacher asked her to paint it.

The teacher asked Claire to paint the mural.

When you're thirsty to emphasize a noun or a pronoun!

Intensive Sensation

From Concentrated Intensive Pronouns

Includes daily recommended allowance of these intensive pronouns: myself, ourselves, yourself, himself, herself, itself, yourselves, and themselves.

64 FL. OZ. (2 QTS) 1.89 L

Pass the Pronoun Punch, Please!

Skill Identifying special kinds of pronouns

Spotlight special kinds of pronouns with an activity that pours on the learning! Divide the class into small groups. Distribute the materials listed. Also assign each group a pronoun type: demonstrative, reflexive, indefinite, interrogative, or intensive (see page 22). Then direct students to follow these steps:

1. Measure the bottle's circumference or front. Then cut out a new label from construction paper.
2. On the paper, draw a new label that will "sell" your pronoun to people who are thirsty for good grammar. Include a name for your "pronoun punch," a list of pronouns from your category, and information on how the pronouns are used.
3. Decorate the label. Then glue it to the bottle.
4. Share your bottle with the class.

Materials needed for each group: 1 large, empty plastic juice bottle (label removed); glue; construction paper; measuring tape; scissors; markers or crayons.

 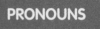

Fishin' for Gold!

Bucky Neer is fishing for gold—goldfish, that is! Help this picky pirate find the goldfish by following the directions below.

Part 1: Use a yellow crayon or marker to color each fish that is labeled with a pronoun.

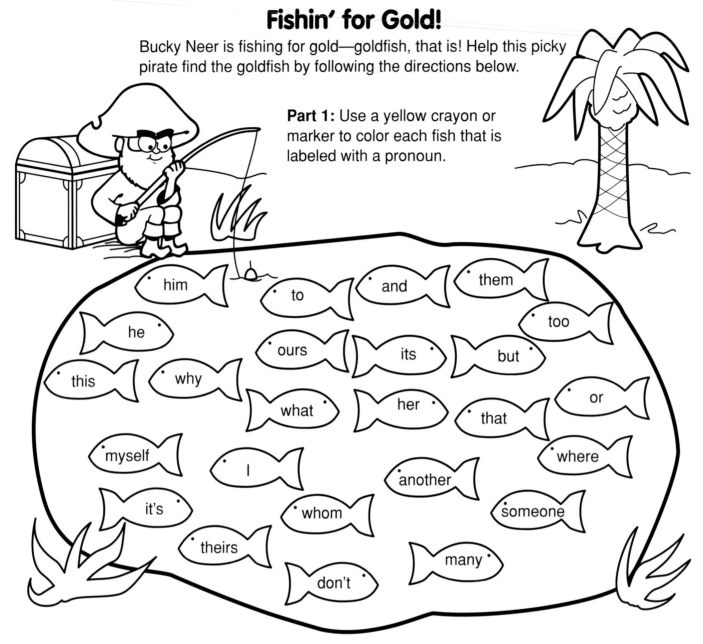

Part 2: Choose five of the pronouns above. On the lines below, write a sentence using each pronoun.

1. _____
2. _____
3. _____
4. _____
5. _____

Bonus Box: On the back of this page, draw ten more fish. Label some of the fish with pronouns that aren't listed on this page. Label the others with words that aren't pronouns. Then give your paper to a classmate. Challenge him or her to color the fish that contain pronouns.

"Gem-Dandy" Pronouns

Find the treasure chest that matches the first letter of your last name. For each gem listed on it, write a sentence that includes that kind of pronoun on your paper. For example, if you use Chest A–H, write one sentence that includes a demonstrative pronoun (1 ruby), two sentences that each include an interrogative pronoun (2 sapphires), four sentences that each include an indefinite pronoun (4 emeralds), and so on.

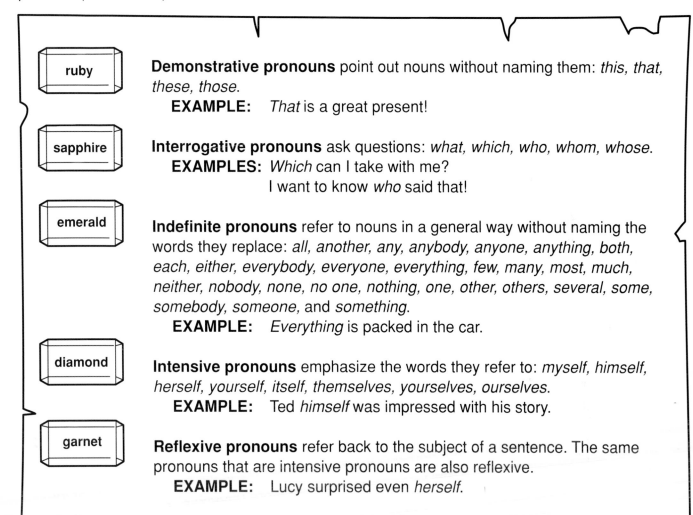

ruby

Demonstrative pronouns point out nouns without naming them: *this, that, these, those.*
> **EXAMPLE:**   *That* is a great present!

sapphire

Interrogative pronouns ask questions: *what, which, who, whom, whose.*
> **EXAMPLES:** *Which* can I take with me?
> I want to know *who* said that!

emerald

Indefinite pronouns refer to nouns in a general way without naming the words they replace: *all, another, any, anybody, anyone, anything, both, each, either, everybody, everyone, everything, few, many, most, much, neither, nobody, none, no one, nothing, one, other, others, several, some, somebody, someone,* and *something.*
> **EXAMPLE:**   *Everything* is packed in the car.

diamond

Intensive pronouns emphasize the words they refer to: *myself, himself, herself, yourself, itself, themselves, yourselves, ourselves.*
> **EXAMPLE:**   Ted *himself* was impressed with his story.

garnet

Reflexive pronouns refer back to the subject of a sentence. The same pronouns that are intensive pronouns are also reflexive.
> **EXAMPLE:**   Lucy surprised even *herself.*

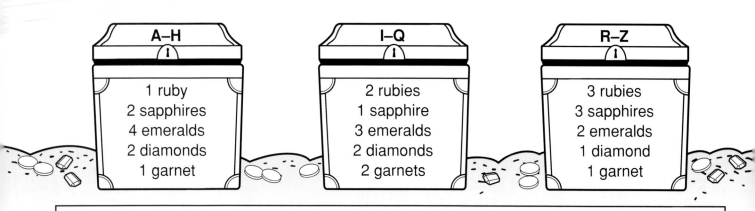

A–H	I–Q	R–Z
1 ruby	2 rubies	3 rubies
2 sapphires	1 sapphire	3 sapphires
4 emeralds	3 emeralds	2 emeralds
2 diamonds	2 diamonds	1 diamond
1 garnet	2 garnets	1 garnet

Bonus Box: Write a paragraph that describes what you'd like to find in a treasure chest. Use at least five pronouns in your paragraph.

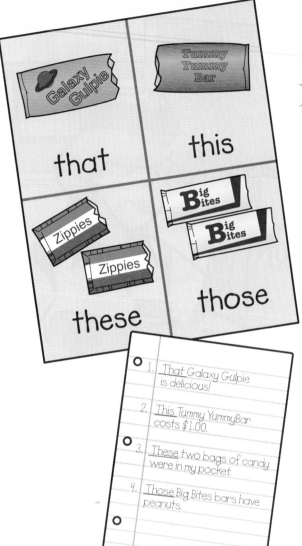

1. That Galaxy Gulpie is delicious!

2. This Tummy Yummy Bar costs $1.00.

3. These two bags of candy were in my pocket.

4. Those Big Bites bars have peanuts.

Point It Out!

Skill Using demonstrative adjectives

Make a point to teach students about demonstrative adjectives with this sweet treat of an activity! Ask each student to bring in one or more candy wrappers. After collecting the wrappers, divide the class into groups of four. Give each group six wrappers, a large sheet of construction paper, a marker, and tape. Each group first uses the marker to divide its paper into four sections. In each section, the group writes a demonstrative adjective and tapes one or more candy wrappers as shown. On notebook paper, the group then writes one descriptive sentence for each section, describing the candy in it and including a demonstrative adjective.

When groups are finished, collect the sentences and display the posters. Read aloud one group's sentences; then challenge the class to identify the poster they describe.

More, Please!

Skill Using comparative and superlative forms

For an appetizing activity on making comparisons with adjectives, pile this idea on your plate! Divide the class into pairs; then give each pair of students two paper plates. Have the twosome label its plates "comparative" and "superlative." Set a timer for one minute; then challenge each pair to list three adjectives that could be used to describe food on each plate as shown. Finally, direct each twosome to write a sentence that uses one of its adjectives to compare two or more different foods. For an eye-catching display, back a bulletin board with a red checkered paper tablecloth. Add some colorful placemats, paper napkins, and the title "Serving Up Adjective Forms!" Then mount the plates and sentences on the board.

comparative
crispier
fresher
more delicious

superlative
tastiest
juiciest
most delectable

French fries are <u>crispier</u> than baked potatoes.

Extra! Extra!

Directions: Read the newspaper article below. Then list the adjectives and the nouns they describe in the blanks. Use the back of this page if you need more space. The first one is done for you.

BONE CASE SOLVED!

Baycity County Jail
257839209

Baycity, ND—A dreadful crime was committed on the dark and gloomy evening of March 17. In the fashionable neighborhood of Kirkwood, a shady criminal was on the loose stealing dog bones. As the tricky thief searched for the most unnoticeable hideaway, the quick-witted inspector was beginning his newest investigation. Cracking the case of the notorious thief would prove to be a difficult task. Who could be digging up and stealing the best dog bones in town?

Finally, the case was solved. The famous bone collector, Dr. Felix Waggingtail, was discovered to be the ruthless robber. His scraggly group of stray dogs was stealing the buried bones in Kirkwood. It seems that the high-class pooches that lived there only eat grilled steak. Life in Baycity can now return to normal. At least, that's what the happy dog owners in Baycity hope!

	Adjective(s)	Noun		Adjective(s)	Noun
1.	*dreadful*	*crime*	11.		
2.			12.		
3.			13.		
4.			14.		
5.			15.		
6.			16.		
7.			17.		
8.			18.		
9.			19.		
10.			20.		

Bonus Box: On the back of this page or on another sheet of paper, draw a large bone. Inside the bone, list ten adjectives you could use to describe a dog.

©2000 The Education Center, Inc. • *Grammar Plus! • Parts of Speech* • TEC2315 • Key p. 48

Note to the teacher: Before having students complete this page, tell them not to list the articles *a, an,* or *the* on the bone. If desired, have students work together in teams to complete this activity.

Appetizing Adjectives

What's on this mouthwatering menu? Proper adjectives! A *proper adjective* is made from a proper noun. It is always capitalized.

Directions: Write each proper adjective beside the correct food on the menu. (The first one has been done for you.) Then write each numbered letter in the matching blank below to read the secret message.

Swiss	Boston	Concord	New England	French
Southern	New York	Belgian	Louisiana	German
French	French	Irish	Canadian	Spanish
Chinese	Georgia	Colombian	Idaho	Maine

* * * * * * * * * * * * *Menu* * * * * * * * * * * * *

I d a h o   potatoes
0   6

___ ___ ___ ___ ___   toast
      13

___ ___ ___ ___ ___ ___ ___   shrimp
16

___ ___ ___ ___ ___   noodles
2

___ ___ ___ ___ ___ ___   cheesecake
                19

___ ___ ___ ___ ___   rice
8

___ ___ ___ ___ ___ ___   coffee
  10

___ ___ ___ ___ ___ ___ ___   fried chicken
            18

___ ___ ___ ___ ___   onion soup
15

___ ___ ___ ___ ___   grapes
      7

___ ___ ___ ___ ___ ___   waffles
20

___ ___ ___ ___ ___   stew
1

___ ___ ___ ___   cheese
3

___ ___ ___ ___ ___ ___   peach
9

___ ___ ___ ___ ___   lobster
        14

___ ___ ___ ___ ___ ___ ___   bacon
          17

___ ___ ___ ___ ___   fries
        4

___ ___ ___ ___ ___   chocolate cake
        5

___ ___ ___ ___ ___   baked beans
11

___ ___ ___ ___ ___ ___ ___ ___   clam chowder
                12

I ' ___ ___ ___ ___ ___ ___ ___ ___ a ___ ___ ___ ___ ___ ___ ___ ___ ___ ___ ___ ___ ___ ___ ___ !
0 5   12 16 1 14 9   20 6 2 19   15 10 18   3 13 7 11 4 17 8

Bonus Box: On the back of this page or on another sheet of paper, write the proper noun from which these proper adjectives are made: *Chinese, Spanish, Colombian, Southern, French, Belgian, Irish, Swiss, Canadian,* and *German.*

Adverbs

An adverb is a word that describes a verb, an adjective, or another adverb.

- **An adverb that describes a verb** answers one of three questions: *how? when?* or *where?*

  EXAMPLES   The ballerina dances **gracefully.** (How does she dance? Gracefully.)
  The ballerina dances **anywhere.** (Where does she dance? Anywhere.)
  The ballerina dances **daily.** (When does she dance? Daily.)

- **An adverb that describes an adjective** usually answers the question *how?*

  EXAMPLE   My dad is **extremely** tall. (How tall? Extremely.)

- **An adverb that describes another adverb** usually answers the question *how?*

  EXAMPLE   My dog ran **exceedingly** quickly. (How quickly? Exceedingly quickly.)

- Adverbs can be expressed in three different forms to show comparisons.

  — An adverb in the **positive** form doesn't make a comparison.

  EXAMPLES   Ann runs **fast.**
  Phil sings **loudly.**

  — The **comparative** is formed by adding *er* to one-syllable adverbs. Use *more* or *less* before most adverbs of more than one syllable.

  EXAMPLES   Ann runs fast, but Bill runs **faster.**
  Phil sings loudly, but Meg sings **more loudly.**

  — The **superlative** is formed by adding *est* to one-syllable adverbs. Use *most* or *least* before most adverbs of more than one syllable.

  EXAMPLES   Bill runs faster than Ann, but Rita runs **fastest.**
  Meg sings more loudly than Phil, but Guy sings **most loudly.**

Adverb Charades

Identifying adverbs that modify verbs

Do your students think that studying parts of speech is no picnic? Change their minds with this nifty activity! Write an action verb, such as *jump,* on the board. Then have one student come to the front of the room and act out the verb. Ask the class to suggest words that describe how the actor jumped (*excitedly, quickly, slowly,* etc.). List the words on the board; then explain that they are adverbs that describe verbs. Next, choose three more students. Write the verb *eat* and the adverbs *frantically, angrily,* and *daintily* on the board. Secretly assign an adverb to each volunteer; then, at your signal, have each of the three actors act out *eat* in the manner of his assigned adverb. Challenge the class to match each adverb to the correct actor. Repeat the activity using the verbs and adverbs shown. Be sure to point out that not all adverbs end in *-ly.* Some—such as *now, later,* and *yesterday*—answer the question *when?* Others—such as *everywhere, here,* and *there*—answer the question *where?*

> **dance:** gracefully, wildly, shyly
> **talk** (on the telephone): seriously, joyously, angrily
> **look:** dreamily, intently, timidly
> **type:** forcefully, lazily, quickly

Well, you sure aren't eating "daintily"!

Adverb ABCs

Identifying adverbs

Make identifying adverbs as easy as ABC with this literature-related activity. Read aloud Graeme Base's book *Animalia* (Harry N. Abrams, Inc.). Each letter in this alphabet book is featured in an alliterative description of an elaborate illustration (such as "eight enormous elephants expertly eating Easter eggs"). Pause after reading each page to ask if students heard an adverb. If they did, write the word on the board. If there is no adverb on the page, challenge students to suggest one that would fit the alliterative text and illustration. As an extension, point out that the phrases used in the book aren't complete sentences; then challenge students to suggest a revision that changes each page's phrase into a complete sentence.

You dance extremely elegantly!

Adverb Comparisons

 Skill **Positive, comparative, and superlative forms of adverbs**

Looking for an activity on adverbs that's beyond compare? Try this one on adverb comparisons. On the board, demonstrate how to write the adverb *fast* in the positive, comparative, and superlative forms *(fast, faster, fastest)*. Repeat using a multisyllabic adverb, such as *loudly (loudly, more loudly, most loudly)*. Explain that the comparative form uses *more* or *less* before adverbs of more than one syllable, while the superlative form uses *most* or *least*.

Next, have each student fold a 12" x 18" sheet of paper into thirds and label each section as shown. Then direct her to write an action verb and the three forms of an adverb in the sections (see the illustration). Finally, have the student illustrate each adverb. Post the drawings on a bulletin board titled "Dare to Compare!"

Positive
runs fast

Comparative
runs faster

Superlative
runs fastest

Modifying Rather Well

Tiger plays phenomenally well!

Skill **Adverbs modifying other adverbs**

Introduce students to adverbs that modify their own kind with this easy-to-do activity. Display these adverbs: *so, too, very, quite, rather, really, awfully, somewhat, extremely, amazingly, exceedingly, extraordinarily, unbelievably*. Explain to students that these adverbs can be used to describe other adverbs and that they answer the question *how?* Ask one student to suggest a sentence that includes an adverb, such as "She sings *loudly*." Have another child add a word from the chart to the sentence, such as "She sings *extremely* loudly." Repeat with several other examples. Then divide the class into groups. Challenge each group to choose a famous person, such as Tiger Woods or Abraham Lincoln. Have the group write five sentences about its famous person (without naming him or her) that each include one of the adverbs displayed. Finally, have each group read its sentences aloud and challenge classmates to identify the celebrity being described.

He hits the ball <u>amazingly</u> <u>hard</u>.
He smiles <u>quite</u> <u>broadly</u>.
He drives the ball <u>extraordinarily</u> <u>far</u>.
He practices <u>unbelievably</u> <u>often</u>.
He putts <u>exceedingly</u> <u>well</u>.

Name That Adverb!

Finding the word an adverb modifies

Help students learn to identify the word an adverb modifies with this cool game. Write this sentence on the board: " 'Don't run!' Vic said suddenly." Ask the class to identify the adverb (suddenly), the word the adverb modifies (said), and the modified word's part of speech (verb). Repeat with other sentences, making sure to feature at least one sentence that includes an adverb modifying an adjective (such as in "My *extremely* beautiful cat is named Fluffy"), and one that includes an adverb modifying another adverb (such as in "She sews *unbelievably* quickly").

Next, give each child a file folder or large folded sheet of construction paper in which to conceal the book she's currently reading. Direct the student to find a sentence in the book that includes an adverb and copy it on her paper. Then divide the class into two teams and follow these steps:

1. Ask a player from Team 1 to read her sentence aloud.
2. Award the following points to Team 2 if it can identify
   - the adverb in the sentence (one point)
   - the word that the adverb modifies (one point)
   - the part of speech of the modified word (one point)
   - the title and author of the book that includes the sentence (two points for each)
3. Repeat Steps 1–2 with a sentence from Team 2.
4. Continue playing until each student has shared her sentence. Declare the team with more points the winner.

> "The adverb is *almost*. It modifies *were*, which is a verb. The title of the book is *Maniac Magee*, and it's written by Jerry Spinelli.

> By the time Maniac looked back, they were almost on him.

Adverb Ants

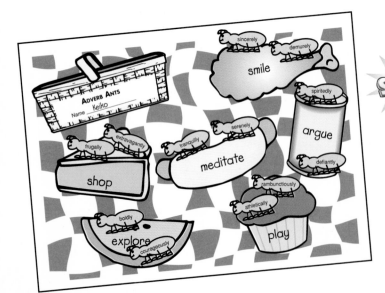

Using descriptive adverbs

Increase your students' use of descriptive adverbs—and pack in a little vocabulary practice—with a ready-to-use activity that doubles as a great rainy-day art activity. Provide each child with a copy of page 37 and the materials listed on it. Then help students complete the page as directed. Display the completed picnic pictures on a bulletin board titled "The Adverb Ants Go Marching!"

ADVERB ANTS

Name _____

Pack a picnic that's full of descriptive adverbs! But get ready—the ants just may come marching!

Materials needed: 2 sheets of construction paper (1 red, 1 white), scissors, glue, 1 sheet of duplicating paper, black marker, black crayon, crayons or markers, dictionary

Steps:

1. Cut the red paper into wavy strips. (Fig. 1)
2. Fold the white paper in half lengthwise. Then cut slits in the paper as shown. (Fig. 2)
3. Unfold the white paper and weave the red strips through the slits (Fig. 3). You'll have some leftover red strips.
4. Put a dab of glue under both ends of each red strip to secure it. Then set this picnic tablecloth aside.
5. On duplicating paper, draw pictures of six picnic foods. Color and cut out the pictures.
6. Use the black marker to write the name of one of these verbs on each food cutout: *shop, explore, argue, smile, meditate, play.*
7. With a black crayon, lightly color each adverb ant below.
8. Cut out the ants. Look up each word in the dictionary. Then place it with the food cutout that is labeled with the verb that it best modifies.
9. When each word has two ants, arrange the food and ants on your tablecloth. Glue the pieces in place.
10. Write your name on the picnic basket cutout. Color and cut out the basket. Then glue it to your tablecloth.

Fig. 1

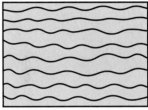

Fig. 2

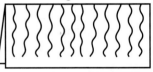

Fig. 3

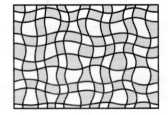

frugally | sincerely | athletically | extravagantly
courageously | tranquilly | demurely | boldly
serenely | rambunctiously | defiantly | spiritedly

Note to the teacher: Use with "Adverb Ants" on page 36. Provide each student with the materials listed.

Adverb Assortment

An *adverb* is a word that describes a verb, an adjective, or another adverb. When an adverb describes a verb, it answers one of these three questions: *how? when?* or *where?*

Directions: Write each adverb in the box on the correct shape below according to the key. (Hint: There should be ten words in each shape.) Then write three additional adverbs in each shape.

anywhere	above	skillfully	outside	fairly
here	fast	always	early	before
noisily	gracefully	near	up	silently
often	rapidly	first	never	well
after	inside	cleverly	there	down
late	soon	softly	far	sometimes

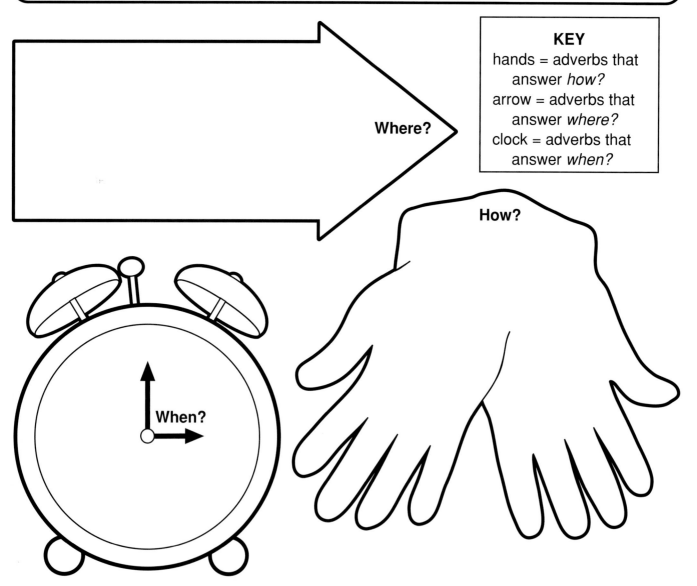

Where?

KEY
hands = adverbs that answer *how?*
arrow = adverbs that answer *where?*
clock = adverbs that answer *when?*

How?

When?

Bonus Box: Think about the best day you've had in the last year. Write a paragraph about the event that uses at least ten of the adverbs listed above.

Prepositions

A preposition is a word that shows the relationship of one word in a sentence to another word.

- **Prepositions** can tell four things: *location* (where something is in relation to something else), *direction* (where something is going), *time,* and *relationship* (between a noun or pronoun and another word).

EXAMPLES	My dad stood **outside** the car. (location)
	My dad walked **toward** the car. (direction)
	My dad waited **until** 10:00 to wash the car. (time)
	My dad washed the car **with** Brian. (relationship)

- A **compound preposition** is two or more words that work together like a one-word preposition. Some examples include *according to, ahead of, along with, as for, instead of, except for,* and *in case of.*

EXAMPLE	Marilyn stood **in front of** me.

- A **prepositional phrase** is a phrase that begins with a preposition and ends with a noun or pronoun known as the object of the preposition. There may also be descriptive words in between the preposition and the object of the preposition.

EXAMPLES	Kelly sits **near me.**
	We went camping **in spite of the terrible weather.**
	Sue drove **over the hill** and **around the forest.**

- The **object of the preposition** is the noun or pronoun that follows a preposition in a prepositional phrase.

EXAMPLES	I put the money <u>inside my coat</u> **pocket.**
	The cat jumped <u>out of the</u> **bag.**

Picturing Prepositions

Start a unit on prepositions with this picture-perfect activity! After introducing this part of speech to the class, have students brainstorm a list of prepositions as you record their responses on a sheet of chart paper. Next, provide each child with a large sheet of construction paper, old magazines, scissors, glue, and markers. Challenge each student to cut out magazine pictures that illustrate prepositions and glue them on his paper collage-style. Then have the child label each picture with an appropriate preposition. Post the picturesque projects and the brainstormed list of words on a bulletin board titled "Picturing Prepositions."

Fishing at Preposition Pond

skill **Identifying compound prepositions**

There's nothing fishy about this easy-to-adapt game that focuses on compound prepositions! For each pair of students, tie together the ends of a 30-inch length of yarn and cut out 16 paper fish. Label each fish with a compound preposition (see the list below). Give each pair of students a yarn circle (the pond) and a set of fish cutouts. Be sure students have access to a timer or a clock with a second hand. Then have each pair follow these rules to play Fishing at Preposition Pond:

1. Place the fish facedown in the pond.
2. In turn, draw a fish from the pond. Use the compound preposition in a sensible sentence before one minute is up.
3. If your partner agrees that your sentence is correct, remove the fish from the pond and keep it. If you aren't able to think of a sentence within the time limit, return the fish to the pond.
4. The game is over when the pond is empty. The player with more fish wins.

according to	away from	in back of	instead of
ahead of	because of	in case of	on top of
along with	except for	in front of	out of
as for	in addition to	in spite of	up to

Popping With Prepositions

Identifying prepositional phrases

Prepositional phrases will be popping out all over during this fun game! Write each preposition shown on a separate index card. Have each child trim a five-inch square of white paper as shown to resemble a piece of popcorn. Then give each student three cards. Direct her to write each preposition in a sentence on one side of her popcorn cutout and her name on the other side.

Divide the class into two teams. Have a Team A player read her first sentence aloud. If a Team B player correctly identifies the prepositional phrase, he wins that cutout. Then Team B reads a sentence. Continue playing until each student has read a sentence. After declaring the team with more cutouts the winner, have students return the sentences to their owners; then play two more rounds with the remaining sentences. At the end of the game, staple the cutouts on a bulletin board titled "Popping With Prepositions."

I went <u>to</u> the store.

Stand <u>underneath</u> my umbrella!

Scott lives <u>near</u> Joey and Ali.

about	behind	from	on	to
above	below	in	onto	toward
across	beneath	in front of	on top of	under
after	beside	inside	out of	underneath
against	between	instead of	outside	until
along	by	into	over	up
among	down	like	past	upon
around	during	near	since	with
at	except	of	through	within
before	for	off	throughout	without

Poetic Prepositions

Identifying the object of the preposition

beside	above	beneath	near	on top of
my house	the clouds	the ocean	my school	the mountain
the car	the bookshelf	the pile	the fish tank	my desk

- above the fluffy, white clouds
- beneath the pile of old, dusty books
- on top of the dark, mysterious, towering mountain

Help students learn to pick out the object of the preposition with this poetic project. Each student lists five prepositions from the list above across the top of an unlined sheet of paper as shown. Below each preposition, he lists five objects that could be used with it. Next, the student circles his three favorite phrases. He then writes each circled phrase on the back of his paper and adds details that make it more descriptive (see the examples). Finally, the student combines his phrases with those of a partner to create a free-verse prepositional poem. After the pair copies the poem on a clean sheet of paper and adds illustrations, compile the completed poems in a class book titled "Prepositional Poetry."

Prepositions Party

Are you a prepositions pro? Find out by completing this page!

Directions: Read the story and fill in the blanks with the prepositions in the gift at the bottom of the page. Then go back through the story and do the following:

- Underline each prepositional phrase.
- Circle each preposition or compound preposition.
- Draw a box around each object of the preposition.

Colin had been looking forward to his birthday for the past month. He had asked his parents if he could have a new bike _____ a party this year. They agreed and bought him a new bike that he really liked. _____ lunch, he went for a ride to show his friends his new bike. He went _____ the school and _____ the park, but none of his friends were there. Colin rode to three friends' houses, but his buddies were not at home. He looked around the town. He even looked behind the bakery where he and his friends liked to sit outside the shop and eat leftover cookies that the baker gave them. He looked by the pond and along the walking path. He rode across the pedestrian mall and between the town garden and bandstand. Colin couldn't find his friends anywhere in town. After an hour, he gave up and sadly headed home with his new bike. His mom was sitting beside his dad on the front porch. She smiled and suggested that Colin put his new bike _____ the garage. Slowly, Colin rolled his bike up to the garage and opened the door. All _____ his friends jumped out and yelled, "Surprise!" Colin laughed and said, "This is the best birthday I've ever had!"

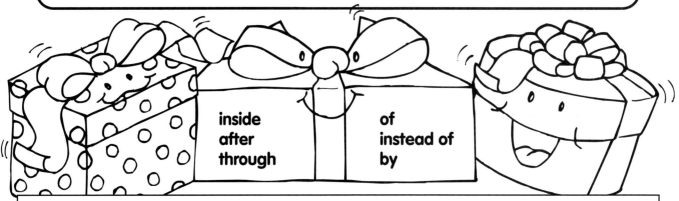

inside
after
through

of
instead of
by

Bonus Box: Write a paragraph describing the best birthday you could ever celebrate (if you could have or do anything you wanted). Include at least six prepositional phrases. Underline the phrases in your favorite color.

Conjunctions & Interjections

 A **conjunction** connects words or groups of words together. An **interjection** is a word or phrase that expresses strong emotions.

- **Coordinating conjunctions** connect words, phrases, and sentences (independent clauses). Examples are *and, nor, but, for, yet, so,* and *or.*

  EXAMPLE   Megan bought apples **and** oranges for our lunch.

- **Subordinating conjunctions** connect dependent clauses to independent clauses. Examples are *after, before, so, till, where, although, for, so that, unless, whereas, as, if, than, until, wherever, as if, once, that, when, whether, because, since, though, whenever,* and *while.*

  EXAMPLE   I won't go **unless** you apologize.

- **Correlative conjunctions** are used in pairs that are split up by other words. Examples are *either/or, both/and, neither/nor, not only/but also, just as/so,* and *whether/or.*

  EXAMPLE   **Not only** is it raining today, **but** it is **also** cold.

- An **adverbial conjunction** connects clauses of equal value. Examples are *accordingly, furthermore, consequently, moreover, hence, however, nevertheless,* and *therefore.*

  EXAMPLE   I hate broccoli; **however,** I love cauliflower.

- An **interjection** shows a strong feeling or emotion. It usually comes at the beginning of a sentence, followed by a comma or an exclamation mark.

  EXAMPLES   **Yippee!** We won the championship!
  Wow, look at the size of that present!

The Conjunction Connection

Using different kinds of conjunctions

Brush up on conjunctions with this partner activity. Give each student a copy of page 46. Have the student color the cover and complete each of the pages as directed. Then have him cut out the pages and staple them in order to create a study booklet. Go over the booklet with students. Then divide the class into pairs. Give each pair a 4" x 18" strip of white construction paper and crayons or markers. Challenge each twosome to design a comic strip that includes at least one example of each kind of conjunction. When everyone is finished, have student pairs swap strips. Have each twosome list each conjunction in the strip on a sheet of paper and then identify its type. Next, have the students return the strip and their answers to the owners for checking. After students swap comics several times, collect the strips and display them on a bulletin board titled "Comic Conjunctions."

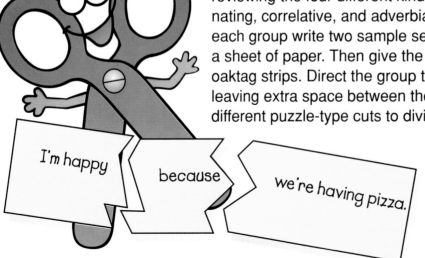

Puzzling Conjunctions

Identifying kinds of conjunctions

Puzzled about how to make learning conjunctions more fun? After reviewing the four different kinds of conjunctions (coordinating, subordinating, correlative, and adverbial), divide the class into groups. Have each group write two sample sentences for each kind of conjunction on a sheet of paper. Then give the group a small paper bag and eight oaktag strips. Direct the group to write each of its sentences on a strip, leaving extra space between the words. Then have the group make different puzzle-type cuts to divide each sentence into its main parts (see the example). Finally, have the group decorate its bag and place the puzzle pieces inside, along with its list of sentences to use as an answer key. Let groups swap bags, complete the puzzles inside, and check their work. Then place the bags at a center for students to check out during their free time.

Thumbs Up!

Identifying kinds of conjunctions

Team 1

Have "thumb" fun studying conjunctions with this kid-pleasin' game. Divide the class into four teams and assign a number to each team. Then direct each student to write four sentences with conjunctions on his paper, label each conjunction according to its type (coordinating, subordinating, correlative, adverbial), and check the sentences with his teammates. While students write their sentences, post four sheets of chart paper on the board. Label each sheet with a team number; then set out several inkpads and fine-tipped markers near the charts.

To play, ask a player from Team 1 to read one of his sentences aloud, name the conjunction, and identify its type. If correct, the player goes to his team's chart, makes a thumbprint on it, and uses the markers to turn the thumbprint into a unique creature. If his answer is incorrect and a member of another team can give a correct response, then she places a thumbprint on her team's chart. Continue until each student has shared at least two sentences. Declare the team with the most thumbprints on its chart the winner.

Interjection Collection

Identifying interjections

Jumping june bugs! Here's the perfect activity to help students identify interjections. Mount the title "Our Interjection Collection" on a bulletin board. Then divide students into pairs. Give each twosome a stack of old magazines and newspapers, two or three sheets of construction paper, scissors, and glue. Challenge each pair to cut out examples of interjections from the magazines and newspapers, glue them on construction paper, and then cut around each one to make a starburst shape as shown. After each twosome shares its interjections with the class, mount the cutouts on the bulletin board. To make the display three-dimensional, have students glue a Styrofoam® packing peanut behind each shape and then glue the cutout onto the board.

Name _____

Date _____

Make the Conjunction Connection!

©The Education Center, Inc.

A **conjunction** is a word that connects words or groups of words together. There are four kinds of conjunctions: *coordinating, subordinating, correlative,* and *adverbial.*

2

A **coordinating conjunction** connects words, phrases, and sentences (independent clauses). **EXAMPLE:** *Pepperoni **and** mushrooms are great together on a pizza.*

Your example: _____

_____

_____

and	but	so
nor	for	or
	yet	

3

A **subordinating conjunction** connects a dependent clause to an independent clause. **EXAMPLE:** *Eat your lunch **before** you go out to play.*

Your example: _____

_____

_____

after	for	until	whether
before	so that	wherever	because
so	unless	as if	since
till	whereas	once	though
where	as	that	whenever
although	if	when	while
	than		

4

Correlative conjunctions are used in pairs that are split up by other words. **EXAMPLE:** ***Not only** is Mary fun, **but** she is **also** a great friend.*

Your example: _____

_____

_____

either/or	neither/nor	just as/so
both/and	not only/but also	whether/or

5

An **adverbial conjunction** connects clauses of equal value. **EXAMPLE:** *I hate broccoli; **however,** I love cauliflower.*

Your example: _____

_____

_____

accordingly	hence
furthermore	however
consequently	nevertheless
moreover	therefore

©2000 The Education Center, Inc. • *Grammar Plus!* • *Parts of Speech* • TEC2315

Note to the teacher: Use with "The Conjunction Connection" on page 44. Each student will need scissors, crayons or markers, and a stapler to complete this page.

Answer Keys

Page 8
Answers in the blanks will vary.
Common nouns (besides those in student answers):
river, movie, city, building, country, restaurant, singer, car, president, soda pop, state, island, planet, team, book, holiday, cereal, apple, ocean, continent
Proper nouns (besides those in student answers): Nile, Chicago, France, Shania Twain, Abraham Lincoln, Bermuda, Mars, Labor Day, Macintosh, Atlantic

Page 18

(Crossword puzzle with the following words: WOULD, BEEN, WERE, WAS, MAY, DOES, MARRY, HAD, HELPING · VERBS, BE, HAS, WILL, HAVE, COULD, MUST, and others)

Page 9

Add _s._
trucks
rodeos
clocks
keys

Add _es._
crashes
heroes
foxes
dresses

Change _y_ to _i_ and add _es._
butterflies
pennies
cherries
candies

Change _f_ or _fe_ to _v_ and add _es._
lives
leaves
halves
wolves

Change to an irregular spelling.
men
mice
children
feet

Do not change.
moose
deer
sheep

Page 19
1. began, begun
2. said, said
3. clean, cleaned
4. laugh, laughed
5. sang or sung, sung
6. hide, hidden
7. took, taken
8. wove or weaved, woven
9. write, written
10. jumped, jumped
11. listened, listened
12. caught, caught
13. yell, yelled
14. yawned, yawned
15. chose, chosen
16. spun, spun
17. brought, brought
18. sprang or sprung, sprung
19. watched, watched
20. fly, flown

Note to the teacher: Boxes that should be colored include 1, 2, 5, 6, 7, 8, 9, 12, 15, 16, 17, 18, 20.

Page 10

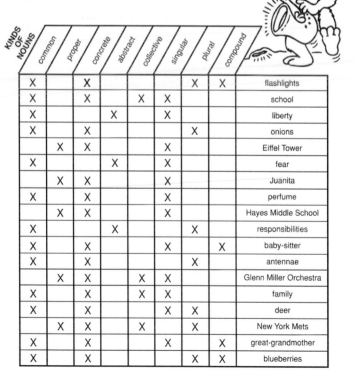

KINDS OF NOUNS	common	proper	concrete	abstract	collective	singular	plural	compound	
	X		X				X	X	flashlights
	X		X		X	X			school
	X			X		X			liberty
	X		X				X		onions
		X	X			X			Eiffel Tower
	X			X		X			fear
		X	X			X			Juanita
	X			X		X			perfume
		X	X			X			Hayes Middle School
	X			X			X		responsibilities
	X		X			X		X	baby-sitter
	X		X				X		antennae
		X	X		X	X			Glenn Miller Orchestra
	X		X		X	X			family
	X		X				X	X	deer
		X	X		X		X		New York Mets
	X		X				X	X	great-grandmother
	X		X				X	X	blueberries

Page 26
Sixteen fish should be colored in:

he / what
him / her
them / that
this / I
ours / whom
its / another
myself / many
theirs / someone

Page 31

Adjective(s)	Noun
1. dreadful	crime
2. dark, gloomy	evening
3. fashionable	neighborhood
4. shady	criminal
5. dog	bones
6. tricky	thief
7. most unnoticeable	hideaway
8. quick-witted	inspector
9. newest	investigation
10. notorious	thief
11. difficult	task
12. best, dog	bones
13. famous, bone	collector
14. ruthless	robber
15. scraggly	group
16. stray	dogs
17. buried	bones
18. high-class	pooches
19. grilled	steak
20. happy, dog	owners

Page 37

Answers may vary. Accept all reasonable answers.

argue: spiritedly, defiantly
meditate: serenely, tranquilly
explore: boldly, courageously
shop: frugally, extravagantly
play: athletically, rambunctiously
smile: sincerely, demurely

Page 38

Where?	When?	How?
anywhere	often	noisily
here	after	fast
above	late	gracefully
inside	soon	rapidly
near	always	skillfully
outside	first	cleverly
up	early	softly
there	never	fairly
far	before	silently
down	sometimes	well

Page 32

```
* * * * * * * * * * * * Menu * * * * * * * * * * * *

I d a h o          potatoes      B e l g i a n        waffles
0   6                            20
F r e n c h        toast         I r i s h            stew
  13                              1
L o u i s i a n a  shrimp        S w i s s            cheese
16                                3
C h i n e s e      noodles       G e o r g i a        peach
2                                 9
N e w   Y o r k    cheesecake    M a i n e            lobster
          19                            14
S p a n i s h      rice          C a n a d i a n      bacon
8                                        17
C o l o m b i a n  coffee        F r e n c h          fries
10                                      4
S o u t h e r n    fried chicken G e r m a n          chocolate
            18                          5               cake
F r e n c h        onion soup    B o s t o n          baked
15                                    11               beans
C o n c o r d      grapes        N e w   E n g l a n d clam
        7                                      12       chowder
```

```
 I 'm   G o i n g   B a c k   F o r   S e c o n d s !
 0  5   12 16 1 14 9  20 6 2 19  15 10 18  3 13 7 11 4 17 8
```

Bonus Box:

Chinese: China
Spanish: Spain
Colombian: Colombia
Southern: South
French: France

Belgian: Belgium
Irish: Ireland
Swiss: Switzerland
Canadian: Canada
German: Germany

Page 42

Colin had been looking forward to his birthday for the past month. He had asked his parents if he could have a new bike **instead of** a party this year. They agreed and bought him a new bike that he really liked. After lunch, he went for a ride to show his friends his new bike. He went by the school and through the park, but none of his friends were there. Colin rode to three friends' houses, but his buddies were not at home. He looked around the town. He even looked behind the bakery where he and his friends liked to sit outside the shop and eat leftover cookies that the baker gave them. He looked by the pond and along the walking path. He rode across the pedestrian mall and between the town garden and bandstand. Colin couldn't find his friends anywhere in town. After an hour he gave up and sadly headed home with his new bike. His mom was sitting beside his dad on the front porch. She smiled and suggested that Colin put his new bike **inside** the garage. Slowly, Colin rolled his bike up to the garage and opened the door. All **of** his friends jumped out and yelled, "Surprise!" Colin laughed and said, "This is the best birthday I've ever had!"